EARLY BOOKS ON CRICKET

Dedicated to
LESLIE GUTTERIDGE

*who refuses to accept
that he knows more about
cricket books than anybody else*

The Bowler from *The Cricket Field*, by James Pycroft (1851)

EARLY BOOKS

on

CRICKET

by

DAVID RAYVERN ALLEN

LONDON: EUROPA PUBLICATIONS

First published 1987

EUROPA PUBLICATIONS LIMITED
18 BEDFORD SQUARE
LONDON, WC1B 3JN, ENGLAND

Allen, David Rayvern
Early books on cricket.
1. Cricket—Bibliography
I. Title
016.79635'8   Z7514.C7

I.S.B.N. 0 946653 26 7

Printed by Staples Printers Rochester Limited, Love Lane, Rochester, Kent.

CONTENTS

Preface
page 7

Collecting Early Cricket Books
page 9

Bibliographical Notes on Early Books
page 47

Index
page 122

THE AUTHOR

David Rayvern Allen has worked as a producer for both BBC Radio and Television for many years and continues to do so, especially within the area of music.

Having gained many awards as a producer, he still finds time to write and edit books. These include: *A Song for Cricket*; a biography of C. Aubrey Smith; four anthologies of John Arlott's broadcasts and writings; *Cricket on the Air*; and *The Punch Book of Cricket*. He also contributes to *Wisden's Cricket Monthly* and other cricket magazines and journals while retaining the distinction of being the only person known to have been bowled first ball by a nonagenarian in the nets at the Hollywood Cricket Club.

David Rayvern Allen lives with his wife, two children and pets in Hertfordshire.

PREFACE

There is usually nothing more counter-productive for an author than to think about finishing a book before he has begun it. Almost always, such wish-fulfilment is nothing more than that, but in this case a decision had to be made concerning the juncture at which one could legitimately end the 'early' period designated by the title. Initially, it seemed that a convenient point would be the arrival of John Wisden's Almanack in 1864; however, further consideration led to the conviction that the period should end with the publication of the first separately printed bibliography of cricket, by Alfred Gaston, in 1895 which has, at least, a degree of connaturalness on its side.

Any publication that ventures, however gingerly, beyond one of the perimeter fences that surround the minefield of cricket bibliography is virtually certain to owe a considerable debt to E. W. Padwick's invaluable compilation produced on behalf of the Cricket Society. Nevertheless, it should be made clear that this small volume does not try to emulate, even to a minute degree, that *magnum opus*. Rather, it was felt that a more discursive approach to an important, if somewhat neglected, area of collecting should be undertaken, if only to collate between two covers strands of information that tend to lie hidden within books and manuscripts on other subjects.

As is to be expected, many of the items listed in the pages that follow are difficult to obtain and commensurately are able to attract nineteenth-century prices. That is to say, of course, they command a price which an antiquarian or specialist bookseller feels is commercially expedient in the twentieth century for a volume that was born before Victoria died. A number of such volumes are noted herein; on their own, perhaps, they are insubstantial in size and content, which is often the case with many of the more expensive items. Be that as it may, it should be recognized that their innate value derives from their reflecting the historical and sociological growth of cricket during that time. Quite often, the booklets (which would generally be a more accurate term) were conceived solely for functional purposes and therefore it is unrealistic to assess them on purely literary grounds: that is not to suggest they are any less attractive as an acquisition.

It would be foolish to aim for, let alone to claim, comprehensiveness in the bibliographical section: the flood of titles with a cricket interest washes over too many archipelagos for that. However, it is reasonably safe to believe that, up to around 1850, there are not many omissions of books devoted entirely to the game. With a few notable exceptions, deliberate avoidance has been made of the innumerable editions of the laws of cricket; there is a remarkably coherent and easily accessible book on the subject by R. S. Rait Kerr. One readily admits a few indulgences in the rarefied realms of manuscript holdings and broadsheets (which are too fascinating not to mention) though, by and large, there has been little straying from the straight and narrow with regard to fringe material. Having raised that point, let me immediately crave temporary immunity from its criteria and place as an appetizer five choice dishes that surely qualify as fundamental fringe; each contains intriguing particles of cricket: 'The Percy Anecdotes' (1821); 'Peacock's Polite Repository' (1826); 'The British Angler's Instructor' by John Cheek (1855); 'The Life of Richard Linsell, the Essex Cricketer, Pedestrian, and Quoit Player — by a Friend' (*c.* 1850); and 'Mockett's Journal' (1836), where we learn that 'The word cricket is of Hebraic origin; the popularity of the game is from the Jews who communicated it to the Romans. In addition to this, Virgil had introduced a game at cricket in his description and Popingus Croesus, a celebrated patrician, lent his title to those boundaries which we still know by the name of Popping Crease? [*sic*]'

All that is left is to take this welcome opportunity of expressing gratitude to a number of kindly souls. John McKenzie provided factual information in the preparation of this exercise and also made available a quantity of rare books from his own library for the purpose of illustration. Hal Cohen, Stephen Green, Leslie Gutteridge, Robert Harragan, Michael Lucy, Alan Oliver, John Pawsey, Diana Rait Kerr, Trefor Rendall Davies, Michael Salzman, Bertram Wakley, Tony Winder, Martin Wood and the staff at the Staples Rochester printing works, all gave necessary assistance and inspiration in various ways; and to each and every one go my heartfelt thanks. They also serve who wait for the word . . .

David Rayvern Allen

COLLECTING EARLY
CRICKET BOOKS

Early References

'Have you any cricket books?' The enquiry of a hopeful buyer invariably draws a half-smiled response from the bookseller, however wearied he may be by the oft-repeated question. He too, by profession, relishes escapism. Does not everybody? So the would-be acquirer is soon to realise that the ransacked shelves speak literally volumes for the happy captivation and solace of winter hours spent by the fireside reliving the warmth of summer, the sound of bat and ball and the smell of the linseed.

Yet where should we start, especially as there are so many directions in which to go? Conveniently, the literature of the game — if, by that, one loosely includes annuals of match results, constitutional booklets and treatises on technique — has been generated for about the last two hundred years. During that time cricket has probably attracted more words to the press than any other single sport, and almost certainly will continue to do so. However, it is cautionary to record that, for collectors young both in years and in spirit, the ever-increasing flood of titles from the publishing houses will surely soon engulf the pockets of those who are accustomed to react obediently to the colour of their bank balances.

Having noted that two hundred years is roughly the period of cricket book writing, let us not forget the many references in print and picture that antedate that time. The sophisticated game that we know today unfolded in very basic form on Kentish weald, Sussex down and further afield. Social historians have built entire careers on the story of the ball game, and their theories are numerous and conclusions as diverse. H. J. Massingham, usually a reliable source, perceived that the ball game was 'an official supernatural and ritual envelope of an activity gradually worn away by the centuries, until what was religion became secular, and what was a social mechanism

9

became a human pastime.' So perhaps, after all, one can draw an albeit tenuous connection between the ancient Egyptian tomb painting of about 1599 BC showing Thothmes III striking balls with an olive-wood wand to the goddess Hathor or Isis and, say, Viv Richards smiting them asunder 'down Somerset way' in the 1980s: the crucial difference being that one game was a religious rite praying for rain and the other likely to be watched by a crowd praying irreligiously for the heavens not to open. We will not embark upon the question of whether professional cricket can legitimately be described as a 'human pastime'.

Cricket is likely to have had a clutch of ancient cousins, pastimes with different names, and there are several mediaeval illuminated manuscripts depicting bat and ball games. Bede's **Life of St. Cuthbert,** thought to be *c.* 1120–30 and held at the Bodleian Library, a decretal issued by Pope Gregory IX around 1230 and a mid-13th-century psalter on vellum, in private hands and brought to public notice by 'Wisden Cricket Monthly', are some of the earliest. The Bodleian have also exhibited **Romance of Alexander** (1340), which shows the figures of three tonsured and bare-footed monks, one holding a club in his left hand, and three nuns, one holding a ball in her right hand.

After the solitary mention of 'creag' in Edward I's Wardrobe Accounts for 1300, references to 'creckett' and eventually 'cricket' accumulate from the late 1500s. Half-way through the sixteenth century **Terra Pacis: A True Testification of the Spirituall Lande of Peace** by Hendrick Niclaes (or Nicholas) was published in Cologne; the English translation from low German specifies 'Kricket-staves'. About the same time, in Surrey, 'creckett' was being played that is described as such (for the first time in English, it is claimed) in a Court Book of the Guildford Borough Records (17th January 1598, new style): 'And also this deponent saith that hee being a scholler in the free Schoole of Guldeford hee [John Derrick] and divers of his fellowes did runne and play there at creckett and other plaies . . .'

In the same year as that court hearing, the lexicographer Giovanni Florio produced **A Worlde of Wordes or Most Copious and Exact Dictionarie in Italian and English** that was printed in London. The dictionary contains a reference to 'cricket-a-wicket', though a

C R O

Croſlé: m. ée: f. *Shaken, wagged, faſt moued.*
Croſler. *To ſhake, wag, tremble; quauer, moue faſt; qui-uer, quake.*
Croſlier: m. ere: f. *Shaking, wagging, quaking, trembling.*
Croſliere: f. *A quagmire, bog; or peece of looſſe, and ſoft ground, that ſhakes vnder the feet.*
Croſse: f. *A Croſier, or Biſhops ſtaffe; alſo, a Cricket-ſtaffe; or, the crooked ſtaffe wherewith boyes play at Cricket.*
Donner la Mitre, & la croſſe à. *To authoriſe, or beare out, by the priuiledge of a religious funſtion; to couer with the ſpecinus cl·ake of Religion.*
Eveſque d'or croſſe de bois, croſſe d'or Eveſque de bois: Prov. *The leſſe a Biſhops ſtaffe, the more his vertue, ſhines; pompe firſt corrupted Prelacie.*
Croſſer. *To play at Cricket.*
Aller ou envoyer croſſer. *To ſend one packing, to bid him goe ſhake his eares.*
Croſſette: f. *A ſlip of a tree, or plant; See* Crocette.

C R (

Eau croupante; *puddle n*
Croupe. *as* Crope; *the top c riumpe, or crupper peece.*
La croupe du dos. *The rid*
Vn chien aſsis ſur la crot taile, or buttocks.
Porter en croupe. *To carr*
Croupeton. vn lievre eſtan *vpon her buttocks (as ſhe do lieſe)and raiſes her ſelfe ther of a feather.*
Croupi: m.ie: f. *as* Croupy
Eau Croupie. *Standing w, as that of lakes, puddles, &c*
Croupie. chaſſer à la croup *lieſe, and then courſe her n*
Croupiere de cheval. *A hor*
Croupir. *To crooch, bow, ſi alſo, to reſt, or grow idle; j place.*

Two early references to cricket in Randle Cotgrave's *Dictionarie of the French and English Tongues* (1611).

few assiduous researchers interpret this as meaning sex and not the game of gentlemen. In 1611, Randle Cotgrave's **Dictionarie of the French and English Tongues,** printed by Adam Islip, describes a 'Cricket-staffe' as 'the crooked staffe wherewith boyes play at cricket.' There are other definitions of the game, and also of club-ball, to be found in the dictionaries of Skinner (1671), Miege (1688), and then of Jamieson and Bailey in the succeeding centuries.

With regard to the recognized literature of the 17th century and before, cricket had managed to find its way onto the pages of Timb's **School Days of Eminent Men; The Works of Rabelais** by Sir Thomas Urquhart; **Angliae Notitia,** by Chamberlayne; and **Mysteries of Love and Eloquence or the Arts of Wooing and Complementary** by Edward Phillips, a nephew of John Milton.

11

There is even an attribution to be found in **The Voyages and Travels of the Ambassadors from the Duke of Holstein to the Grand Duke of Muscovy, and the King of Persia** by Adam Olearius. John Davies's adjacent translation discloses how Persian grandees kept fit in 1637: 'They play there also at a certain Game, which the Persians call Kuitsckauken, which is a kind of Mall, or Cricket.' The comparison is the translator's own.

A memorable starting-point for 18th-century cricket writing was in Latin verse with **In certamen pilae** (1706) from **Musae Juveniles** by William Goldwin, who had gone up to King's, Cambridge from Eton in 1700 and who was later to become headmaster of Bristol Grammar School. Goldwin had a devoted wife who could not bear the thought of living alone and she expired in a most timely fashion within a half an hour of his death. Although there had been a probable reference to the boys of Winchester playing cricket, in a Latin poem of the 1640s by Robert Matthew, Goldwin's **In certamen pilae** was the first full description of a match that has been found. Apparently, the publication mouldered for over two hundred years in 'a literary lumber-room' until finally, in 1922, the editor of 'Etoniana' resurrected it for posterity with the addition of an English translation by Harold Perry.

The antics of cricketers and the idiosyncrasies of the game itself now began to serve as a useful metaphorical tool in all sorts of literary effusions — magazines, mock operas, plays, pamphlets, tracts, broadsheets, books, booklets of verse — and it is relevant to list the titles of some of these, if only to indicate that cricket can lie in surroundings 'passing strange': **A Rod for Tunbridge Beaus, bundl'd up at the Request of the Tunbridge Ladies** (1701), **Lewis Baboon turned Honest, and John Bull Politician, being the Fourth Part of Law is a Bottomless Pit** (1712), **The Devil and the Peers; or, the princely way of Sabbath breaking** (1712), **Memoirs of the lives, intrigues and comical adventures of the most famous gamesters and celebrated Sharpers** (1714), **Pills to Purge Melancholy** (1719), **The Rape of Helen** (1737), **The Dunciad** (1742), **Love at First Sight, or the Gay on a Flutter** (1750) and **The Torpedo, a poem to the Electrical Eel, addressed to Mr. John Hunter surgeon: and dedicated to the Right Honourable Lord Cholmondeley** (1777). This last-named poem refers to the Duke of Dorset and carries an amusing footnote: 'Everyone knows the attachment of the Duke of Dorset to cricket; the following anecdote will prove it. Two Clergymen were candidates for a living on his Grace's presentation, which he bestowed on the best batsman.'

Cricket inevitably attracted facetious comment, and the humorous side of the game, laced with its ever-present potential for extraordinary happening, has, over the years, been exhaustively plumbed with both the spoken and the written word. In July 1785 an article was penned in letter form to the editor of 'The Rambler's Magazine', describing an incident at a recent match at White Conduit Fields that was bizarre in the extreme. Under the title, 'The Cricket Ball Lost in a Furze Bush', the writer, pseudonymed 'a lover of the wicket', recounts how 'one of the balls was sent with such force and fury, that a lady who thought herself perfectly secured by distance from the scene of action, received it in a very improper place. As if enamoured of the lady's charms, it flew with such eagerness as to make her lose the centre of gravity and fall upon her back. For some time the ball was not to be found, on which the usual cry of "a lost ball" was vocifered [*sic*] — but at length it came to light, and was taken from between the lady's legs, though not till after the adverse party had lost a notch by the delay . . .'

The status of cricket improved during the 1700s. Good Queen Anne had repealed the Act whereby those playing in an organized game were liable to a £10 fine and two years in prison, but, more influentially, the noble lords of the realm had started to take an active interest that matched that of the 'lower orders'. Nevertheless, even the imprimatur of the aristocracy had not managed to silence a few puritans. One John Geere of Guildford lumped cricket in with much less worthy pursuits in a diatribe that gave **Serious Considerations on plays, games, and other fashionable diversions. Shewing the sinfulness and dangerous tendency thereof** (1763).

Geere would most certainly have disapproved of James Love (Dance), whom he would have regarded as a dissolute 'rogue and vagabond'. Love had gone on the stage as a 'comedian' after being declared bankrupt following a privileged education at St. John's, Oxford. He was the son of the architect who designed the Mansion

CRICKET.

A N

HEROIC POEM.

ILLUSTRATED

With the Critical Obfervations of
SCRIBLERUS MAXIMUS.

L O N D O N:

Printed for W. BICKERTON, at the *Gazette*, in the
Temple-Exchange, near the *Inner Temple-Gate*, *Fleet-Street*.
[Price One Shilling.]

See item 2 of the Bibliographical Notes

House and he is remembered today solely because of his panegyric **Cricket: an heroic poem. Illustrated with the critical observations of Scriblerus Maximus** (1744). The poem, written in couplets, describes 'in true Virgilian manner' how Kent beat All-England in 'the greatest cricket match ever known' at the Artillery Ground in London. This piece reached five editions in twenty-six years, and a sixth followed in 1922, edited by that legendary cricket 'polymath', F. S. Ashley-Cooper.

Much early writing on the game was confined to verse and, not unnaturally, the baldly stated results of matches found a more refined level and new outlet in poetic licence. Kent and Surrey were two of the most powerful teams in the land and so we have **Surry Triumphant or the Kentish-Men's Defeat** (1773), a ballad by the Rev. John Duncombe, that was a parody of a game played at Bishopsbourne Paddock, and also its sequel **The Kentish Cricketers**, a poem by John Burnby in the same year. Five years later, 'a poetical and Familiar Epistle, address'd to Two of the idlest Lords in his Majesty's Three Kingdoms', entitled **The Noble Cricketers**, was published by J. Bew. The anonymous satirist chose the Duke of Dorset and the Earl of Tankerville as his main victims and berated them for devoting too much time to cricket. He took 22 pages to make his point.

We should be grateful that it took Ferdinando Fungus, Gent., the *nom de plume* of one Williams of Wadham College, only 'twenty-four cantos' to complete his less than serious 'gymnastic poeme' to **The Cryketeers** (1790). The self-effacing versifier ascribes the work to his esteemed friend, Edmunde Byrk, Esquire, and after that there is little more that need be said.

An unexpected and totally different view of this mostly pre-Hambledon period of cricket in England became available when the letters of the Swiss traveller, Monsieur César de Saussure, to his family, were published in 1902 under the title **A Foreign View of England in the Reigns of George I and George II,** having been translated and edited by Madame Van Muyden. It is a befitting reminder that there were at least half a dozen diarists at the end of the 17th century or during the 18th who made reference, either singularly or plurally, to cricket in their writings. Four of them certainly deserve identifying.

15

Firstly, there was the naval chaplain, Henry Teonge, who kept a diary of his service on board His Majesty's ships 'Assistance', 'Bristol' and 'Royal Oak' between 1675 and 1679. His entry for 6th May 1676 is important because of the early date and unlikely place: 'This morning early (as it is the custom all summer longe) at the least 40 of the English [residents], with his worship the Consull, rod out of the cytty [Aleppo] about 4 miles to the Greene Platt, a fine vally by a river syde, to recreate them selves. Where a princely tent was pitched: and wee had severall pastimes and sports, as duck-hunting, fishing, shooting, handball, krickett, scrofilo; and then a noble dinner brought thither, with greate plenty of all sorts of wines, punch and lemonads; and at 6 wee returne all home in good order, but soundly tyred and weary.'

The temperature in Syria is generally warmer than that of the East Coast of America, so it could not have been fear of fatigue or sunstroke that caused William Byrd and his friends to rise at 6 a.m. in order to play cricket hard by the James river in Virginia. Although Marion Tinling's deciphered transcription of Byrd's diary consistently refers to the games as 'cricket', the fact that often unequal sides of, say, four against three played one another, as well as other inferences, suggests a kinship closer to different pastimes. Byrd had spent a number of years in England as a pupil at Felsted School and as a member of the Middle Temple, and at the time of his writing the first part of his 'secret diary' between 1709 and 1712 he was resident back in America at Westover, occupied in the Council of State, and as a receiver-general of the royal revenues. This urbane colonial diplomat admits more than once to having won a 'bit' (an eighth of a Spanish dollar) on the results of those morning games.

Byrd's first wife, Lucy, to whom he was married at the time of his diary, was the daughter of the rakish Daniel Parke, then Governor of the Leeward Islands; and, coincidentally, our next diarist, John Baker, also held office on those islands as Solicitor-General. Baker, born in the year that the initial part of Byrd's diary ceased, had another connection with Byrd, as a member of the Middle Temple. His diary, which is mostly concerned with the time when he lived in the Home Counties, provides a fascinating insight into the difficulties of travelling in pre-industrial Britain; there are many colourful accounts of matches witnessed over a twenty-year period from 1758.

At one point Baker set up home at Horsham, not too far from East Hoathly, where a shopkeeper called Thomas Turner lived, mostly in a state of inebriation. In his sober moments Turner made manuscript notes of cricketing encounters that he had seen in 1763 and 1764; the diary was later edited by Florence Turner and published with an introduction from J. B. Priestley in 1925. In fact, the diaries of all four men were either first published or reprinted in the 20th century.

By the end of the 18th century, cricket had become more organized and, to a degree, centralized. The focus generally was on Lord's or on matches that had associations with the Marylebone Club. Teams in Kent and Sussex, and at Hambledon in Hampshire, had in turn had their 'glory' years but the nursery slopes now conceded to the jurisdiction and maturity of official bodies at Headquarters. Laws were constituted and published — as they had been before, of course — but now the prevalent idea was that there should be a consistent code throughout the land. The scores of matches were printed and produced, while the pen on paper took the place of the notch on wood. As the 19th century began, the first books devoted solely to cricket, and containing prose instead of poetry, started to appear.

Pre-Wisden

Soon after the Marylebone Cricket Club had become established in Dorset Square on the Portman Estate their scorer, Samuel Britcher, produced the first of a **Complete List of all the Grand Matches of Cricket**. The yearly scores ran from 1790 to 1805 and comprised fifteen volumes in all, the last two years, compiled by Stanhope and Graham, being compressed into a single issue.

To Britcher, 'a highly educated individual' according to his contemporaries, goes the credit for compiling the first cricket annuals and, indeed, the first regular series of scores. True, the printed scorebook of the Old Hambledon Club, which seems to have long disappeared from view, is likely to have preceded Britcher, but those scores would have concentrated only on the matches that involved the Club, whereas Britcher spread his net wide, collating details that could not have been easy to gather in those days of relatively poor communication.

In 1799, W. Epps, who ran a press in Troy-Town, a district of Rochester in Kent, arranged and printed **A Collection of all The Grand Matches of Cricket played in England within twenty years, viz from 1771 to 1791, never before published.** Epps knew of Britcher — they are likely to have met, if not before, at a double wicket match in Rochester during the summer of 1799 — and in his 'Apology', by way of a preface, he acknowledges that the existence of the Britcher scores 'obviates the necessity of continuing his publication to a subsequent period.'

A notable patron of Kent cricket was Stephen Amherst, who had enlisted the services of a 'crack' player of the time, Thomas Boxall, not only for 'grand matches' in the county but also as a personal coach. Amherst kept an eye on Boxall, even when the latter had retired — he was instrumental in Boxall's obtaining the post of tidewaiter on the Thames at Purfleet — and it may well have been his suggestion that induced Boxall to produce an instructional handbook, if only for financial reasons, when the player's time ahead in cricket looked limited.

Boxall, who was resident at 27 John Street, Thomas Place, Dockhead during the preparation of the book, eventually vanished into obscurity and there are similar cloudy areas surrounding the subsequent supposed piracy of 'his' work. In order to explain what might have happened it is necessary to enlarge on a little of the background.

Boxall's **Rules and Instructions for Playing at the Game of Cricket** was printed in 1801 by Harrild and Billing at the Blue Coat Boy printing office at Russell Street in Bermondsey. Robert Harrild had an inventive mind; he introduced several new working aids to simplify the transfer of words onto printing blocks and he also assisted John Baxter in experiments of a similar kind. Now, when Baxter's ill health forced him to move down to the South Coast he took the opportunity to open his own printing and publishing house in Lewes, where, incidentally, the firm still remains.

CRICKET.

A

COLLECTION

OF ALL

THE GRAND MATCHES

OF

CRICKET,

PLAYED IN ENGLAND,

WITHIN TWENTY YEARS;

VIZ.

FROM 1771, TO 1791,

NEVER BEFORE PUBLISHED.

ARRANGED, AND PRINTED,

BY W. EPPS,

TROY-TOWN, ROCHESTER.

1799.

See item 10 of the Bibliographical Notes

From Lambert's *Instructions and Rules for playing the Noble Game of Cricket* (see illustration opposite).

In 1809, seven years after setting up in the town, Baxter gave his name to a 12-page pamphlet of the corrected laws of the game and then, in 1816, published **Instructions and Rules for playing the Noble Game of Cricket, as practised by the most eminent players** by William Lambert. It was this publication that attracted possibly unjustified accusations, as there were strong resemblances between Boxall's handbook and Lambert's booklet.

As a result, Baxter has been labelled 'an unscrupulous speculator' and Lambert denounced as 'a plagiarist', though it is unlikely that either was guilty. We have ample evidence to prove that both Boxall and Lambert were skilled performers on the cricket field; however, there is nothing to suggest that they were not unschooled novices under the literary lamp. John Baxter, on the other hand, was an educated man with a decided feeling for words which, after all, was

INSTRUCTIONS AND RULES

FOR

PLAYING THE

NOBLE GAME OF CRICKET,

AS PRACTISED BY THE MOST EMINENT PLAYERS,

Containing a variety of directions little known to Players
in general.

ILLUSTRATED BY AN

Elegant Copper=Plate Engraving,

Exhibiting the Players in the Field,

◆

TO WHICH ARE SUBJOINED

THE LAWS OF THE GAME,

WITH ADDITIONS AND CORRECTIONS,

◆

BY WILLIAM LAMBERT.

◆

SUSSEX PRESS, LEWES:

*Printed and Published by J. Baxter, and sold in London by
Baldwin & Co. Paternoster Row, and all Booksellers.*

1 8 1 6.

See item 17 of the Bibliographical Notes

; 49

RULES & INSTRUCTIONS

F O R

P L A Y I N G

AT THE GAME

O F

C R I C K E T,

AS PRACTISED BY THE MOST EMINENT PLAYERS.

TO WHICH IS SUBJOINED

The Laws and Regulations

O F

CRICKETTERS,

As Revised by the Cricket Club at Mary-le-bone.

BY T. BOXALL.

LONDON.

Printed by Harrild and Billing, at the Blue-Coat Boy
Printing Office, *Russell Street, Bermondsey :*
And sold by all Booksellers in Town and Country.

(1800)

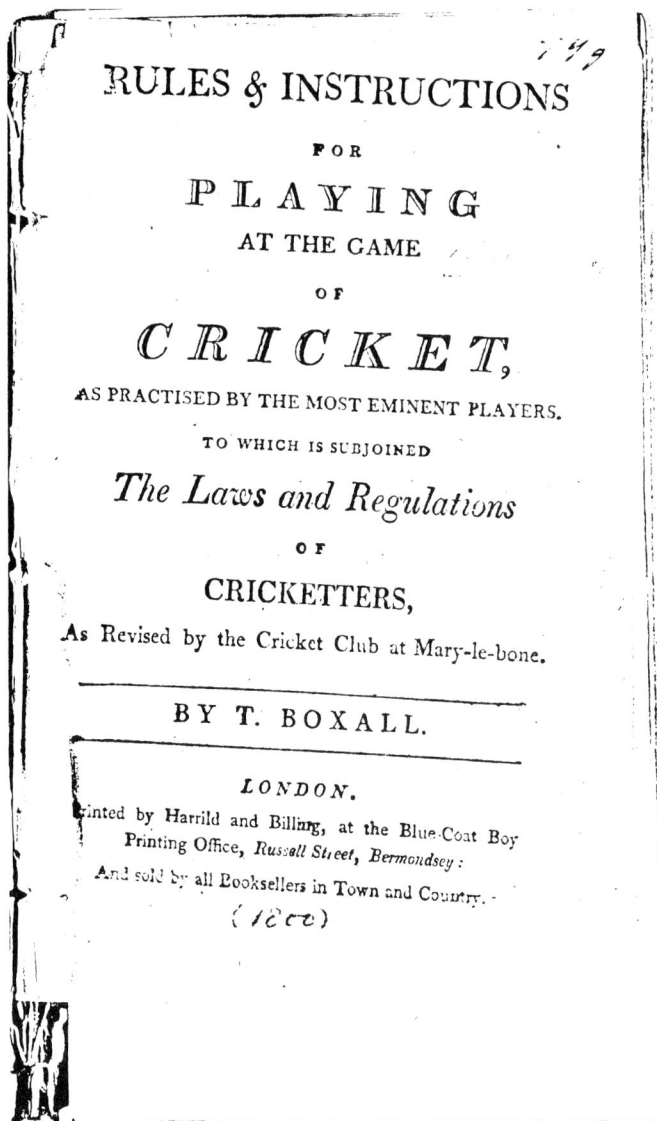

See item 11 of the Bibliographical Notes

part of his business. He had amicable relations with Robert Harrild, who had relinquished his half of the partnership with Billing in 1804 — Billing printed the third edition of Boxall on his own from Star Corner, Bermondsey — and later their ties were to become even closer when Baxter's son, George, married Harrild's daughter, Mary. There is another connection in that Harrild, located in new premises at Great East Cheap, is advertised on the title page of the Lambert book as one of the half-dozen principal suppliers.

Credulity is not stretched by speculating that Baxter assisted in compiling Boxall's work and almost certainly had a hand in Lambert's. Publishing techniques rely on fundamental precepts in any era and the name of a 'star' player on the cover does not harm sales. Accepting that Boxall, who in his dedication to the Marylebone Club had 'devoted a Portion of Time to pening [*sic*] those Articles which may guide the inexperienced . . .', does not hamper the theory of a 'ghost'. And when it came to Lambert's work, Baxter, in his preface to the many editions that were to follow, adopted a most proprietorial tone: 'J. Baxter feels himself particularly obliged to his friends and the public for the very handsome patronage bestowed on the former Editions of the above . . .' Well might he have felt pleased. In 1865, M. A. Lower, F.S.A., writes that 'it was extremely popular, upwards of 300,000 copies having been sold.'

Another celebrated player, who is now chiefly remembered for his recording of cricketing exploits, is Henry Bentley. Bentley, a respected umpire after finishing as a player, lived close to Lord's at 12 Grove Street, Lisson Grove, where he could often be heard practising on the flute, his principal hobby. In 1823 he produced **A Correct Account of all the Cricket Matches which have been played by the Marylebone Club and all other Principal Matches from the Year 1786 to 1822 inclusive.** Bentley's book was certainly the bulkiest and most comprehensive tome on cricket to date (that we know of), though that indefatigable collator, Arthur Haygarth, did wonder whether some of the scoring details included were all that correct.

There were two supplements to the work, firstly **An Account of the Principal Cricket Matches played in the year 1823,** issued in the latter part of the same year, and then **A Correct Account of all the Cricket Matches which have been played by the**

Marylebone Club, and all other Principal Matches in the Years 1824 and 1825, being an appendix published in 1826. Interestingly, more or less the same period, 1786–1823 plus other years, was covered in two handwritten volumes by J. Masters.

In 1826, there appeared an item which is now extremely scarce; in fact only once has it surfaced in the catalogues of cricket literature during the last twenty years, and that was at the Hodgson sale of part of the collection of that legendary collector, J. W. Goldman. **The Cricketers' Pocket Companion . . . dedicated to the Members of the Cricket Clubs of the United Kingdom by a batsman,** printed for William Cole, is now housed in the British Library (or rather, that particular copy of it is). Cole was a prominent editor and publisher who had offices in the City; it seems to have been his sole foray into the world of cricket. The booklet contains a useful digest of the laws and, as the title implies, was of convenient size to park on the person while watching the match. It is almost certain that Cole's **Companion** is a later edition of **The Cricketer's Pocket Companion** (1818; see items 18 and 19 in the Bibliography), which had been published from the same address (10 Newgate Street).

Cricket was still awaiting its first major literary *opus* and that was to come very shortly, in 1833, but before extolling Nyren it is worth taking a quick audit of some fringe material from the early part of the 19th century that is often overlooked. To do so makes one realise that a consciousness of the game and its possible derivations had spread far wider than is sometimes supposed, and this is reflected in some unlikely sources.

Going back to 1801, we have cricket being described for the first time in Danish in a book of gymnastic and party games by J. Werfel. This in turn is a translation from a German offering five years previously: **Spiele zur Vebung** [*sic*] **und Erholung de Körpers und Geists für die Jugend** ('Games for the Young for the Recreation of Body and Spirit'). Then there is an explanation and illustration in a children's book **Les jeux de jeunes garçons** ('Young Boys' Games'), published in Paris in 1807 by the brothers Noël; a chapter and engravings in another work of the same genre and produced in the same locale, **Les jeux de l'enfance . . .** ('Childhood Games') by Théodore-Pierre Bertin; and **Remarks on Children's Play** published by S. Wood and Sons in New York in 1819.

Cricket became a common theme and illustration in juvenilia: **Tales for Ellen,** Volume 1 in the series, and Mary Elliot's **The Rose** and **The Troubles of Harry Careless, or Going Too Far,** are but three examples from this period. The U.S.A. (Boston this time) provided another peripheral entry in 1809, with the publication of George Augustus Warville's introduction to the games of **Pam-lu, Chess and Cricket;** while back home in England Edmund Hoyle, Richard Johnson, Joseph Strutt and Jehoshaphat Aspin all provided volumes on sports, games and pastimes incorporating cricket to a greater or a lesser extent.

The disastrous fire at Lord's in 1825, which destroyed the pavilion and all the records therein, has made it impossible to estimate with any accuracy the number of early books on cricket irretrievably lost. We know that the manuscripts of patrons like Sir Horace Mann and 'Squire' Paulet disappeared, and probably much else was destroyed. Whatever, for instance, became of a book noted by Alfred D. Taylor, in his **Catalogue of Cricket Literature,** published in 1906? He wrote that '**Norfolk,** a book entirely devoted to cricket, of which I have been unable to ascertain the title', was printed 'by R. Bacon for H. Parsons' in 1811. Recent searches for the name of the book have proved equally unsuccessful, though it is perhaps worth mentioning for any potential researcher, that Richard Mackenzie Bacon first assisted, then succeeded his father, Richard Bacon, as editor of 'The Norwich Mercury'.

In the manuscript field, which is largely outside the scope of this book, there were some exceptional endeavours which resulted in such works as the vellum-bound **Kingscote C.C. Scores** of the early 1820s, the compilation being either directly organized by or overseen by the redoubtable Henry Robert Kingscote, and also **A Match Diary 1824/5** by Edward Harbottle Grimston, one time Member of Parliament for St. Albans and at other times Rector for various parishes in Hertfordshire and Essex. Grimston, whose brother, the Hon. Robert, is far better known in cricket circles, penned his diary as a youngster in his teens and covered a wide geographical area: the manuscript is held at the Hertfordshire Record Office.

One is tempted irreligiously to adapt a Biblical allusion by suggesting that before the word came the manuscript. In the case of the first two outstanding essays at substantial cricket literature

THE YOUNG

CRICKETER'S TUTOR;

COMPRISING

FULL DIRECTIONS FOR PLAYING THE ELEGANT AND
MANLY GAME OF

CRICKET;

WITH A COMPLETE VERSION OF ITS LAWS
AND REGULATIONS:

By JOHN NYREN,

*A Player in the celebrated Old Hambledon Club, and in the
Mary-le-Bone Club.*

TO WHICH IS ADDED,

" The Cricketers of My Time,"

OR,

RECOLLECTIONS OF THE MOST FAMOUS OLD
PLAYERS:

BY THE SAME AUTHOR.

THE WHOLE COLLECTED AND EDITED

By CHARLES COWDEN CLARKE.

LONDON:

PUBLISHED BY

EFFINGHAM WILSON, ROYAL EXCHANGE.

1833.

See item 26 of the Bibliographical Notes

which were put into print, that is undoubtedly true. The Rev. James Pycroft, and before him John Nyren, both benefited from conversations with, and handwritten papers from, the likes of Fennex, Barker, the Rev. Mitford and Ward; Nyren dedicated his book to William Ward though, of course, Nyren had first-hand knowledge of the players and events which are recounted so vividly in **The Young Cricketers Tutor . . . to which is added The Cricketers of My Time** (1833). His collaboration with Charles Cowden Clarke has been the subject of endless speculation over the years, as attempts have been made to decide how much of the work is Nyren's and how much is Clarke's. With the little evidence elsewhere from which to gain enlightenment, it seems that in the manner of the best double acts neither could perform as well on their own. E. V. Lucas made what is likely to be an accurate assessment when he wrote that 'Clarke acted as a reasonably enfranchised stenographer.'

Nyren, born at Hambledon in 1764, was the son of Richard Nyren, the Club's 'general' in the great years. **The Cricketers of My Time** had originally formed an irregular series of articles in a periodical called 'Town', and in book form, together with **The Tutor,** ran to many editions over 150 years. This *locus classicus* of cricket has many relishable passages; chosen at random, here is a description of Tom Walker:

> Tom's hard ungain, scrag-of-mutton frame; wilted, apple-john face . . . his long spider legs, as thick at the ankles as at the hips, and perfectly straight all the way down. Tom was the driest and most rigid-limbed chap I ever knew; his skin was like the rind of an old oak, and as sapless. I have seen his knuckles handsomely knocked about from Harris's bowling, but never saw any blood upon his hands — you might just as well attempt to phlebotomise a mummy.

During Nyren's playing days he was sometimes referred to as 'Hambledon', although the inscriptions in the scorebook of the Homerton Club (1804–1808; a copy is held at Lord's), for whom he often kept wicket, allude to him correctly. How enlightening it would be if Nyren had been tempted to make a comparable record of Benjamin Aislabie's club (which was conceivably in Cowden Clarke's mind when he comments speculatively at the end of his introduction to **The Tutor**), even though it is difficult to imagine that the environs of the capital and its personalities would have proved so rich an inspiration as the character and characters of his own village home.

Rural life and scenery had been studied a decade or so before **The Tutor** in **Our Village** by Mary Russell Mitford. The sketches, in five volumes, including those of village cricket, had originally been serialized in 'The Lady's Magazine' in 1819. They have earned a description as the first major prose on the game.

The other Mitford with cricketing affiliations, the Rev. John, who, incidentally, twice reviewed Nyren's book in 'The Gentleman's Magazine', renewed his connection with the classics of the game in a fortuitous manner. When he was the vicar of Benhall in Suffolk, he provided a roof for a hardy professional of yesteryear, William Fennex, and wisely committed their conversations to paper. He gave this manuscript to James Pycroft, who had obtained a cricket blue at Oxford, and seemed destined to have a career in Law, but had instead chosen a holier order and cloth. Pycroft was so enthused by the Fennex memoirs that he started gathering even more information concerning 'the good old days', and this eventually reached fruition with **The Cricket Field** in 1851. This book was a significant landmark in cricket literature and followed the course set by **The Young Cricketer's Tutor** insofar as it was frequently reprinted.

Pycroft, who was also known as a writer of educational treatises on English Reading and Latin and Greek Grammar, had ventured into print on cricket in 1835 with **The Principles of Scientific Batting. . . .** His later publications in the 1860s included **The Cricket Tutor, Cricketana** and **Reminiscences of the Old Players**; though before that, in 1859, **The Cricket Field,** which had already achieved three editions in Britain, was published in Boston, U.S.A., by the firm of Mayhew and Baker.

This is not as surprising as it may seem for at that time cricket had a healthy following on the East Coast of America and 1859 was, in fact, the year of the first English Cricketers' trip to Canada and the United States. The adventures of the intrepid twelve, who included John Lillywhite and John Wisden in their number (both of whom were soon to put their name to cricket annuals), were ingenuously documented by Fred Lillywhite, who accompanied the

THE

CRICKET FIELD:

OR,

THE HISTORY AND THE SCIENCE

OF

CRICKET.

BY THE AUTHOR OF

" THE PRINCIPLES OF SCIENTIFIC BATTING,"
" RECOLLECTIONS OF COLLEGE DAYS,"
ETC. ETC.

Gaudet . . . . aprici gramine campi. — HOR.

LONDON:
LONGMAN, BROWN, GREEN, AND LONGMANS.
1851.

See item 61 of the Bibliographical Notes

party with his tent as scorer and reporter. His is the first overseas tour chronicle and a picture emerges which is akin to an adventure story.

Mayhew and Baker produced another much smaller cricket item in 1859, **The Cricket Player's Pocket Companion.** This rarity, in essence, is the second edition of **A Manual of Cricket and Baseball,** which had been published the previous year, though for the second edition there is additional material and each sport is allocated a book to itself.

The American public had been served fifteen years earlier by their own edition of **The Cricketer's Handbook** (an appropriation of Tyas), which was produced by Saxton, Pierce and Co. in Boston and Saxton and Miles in New York. This Handbook, containing remarks on the origin of cricket and directions for playing the game together with a print of a Bouvé and Sharp lithograph of a view of Lord's, had been preceded by three English editions. Tyas, who had a business association with Menzies of Edinburgh, had produced two of the editions from his office at 50 Cheapside, London, in 1838, and the third from his new address at Paternoster Row in 1841. They were part of a series of handbooks on diverse sports and occupations ranging from archery and angling to banking and cribbage.

William Mark Clark, wholesale bookseller and prolific publisher, had premises at 17 Warwick Lane, just by Paternoster Row, and a printing press at 10 Red Lion Court, Fleet Street. He must surely have been acquainted with Tyas and his product, for he too marketed a series of sporting handbooks, in this case on pedestrianism and wrestling, boxing and, of course, cricket. **The Cricketer's Handbook . . . in three parts** first came out around 1845 and ostensibly ran to 15 editions, though whether or not Clark found a high number useful as a promotional ploy, to infer demand and thereby increase sales, we will probably never know. Only the first, an unnumbered edition, the 10th, the 14th and the 15th appear to be extant.

Clark's Handbook followed the invariable pattern of all such works by including the latest revision of the laws of the game. Ever since the laws had first been sold in booklet form by W. Reeve in Fleet Street in 1755, there have been innumerable variations and

LORD'S CRICKET GROUND.

THE

𝔊𝔯𝔦𝔠𝔨𝔢𝔱'𝔰 𝔥𝔞𝔫𝔡=𝔅𝔬𝔬𝔨.

CONTAINING

THE ORIGIN OF THE GAME,
REMARKS ON RECENT ALTERATIONS, DIRECTIONS
FOR BOWLING, STRIKING, AND PLACING THE
PLAYERS, AND THE LAWS AS ALTERED
BY THE MARYLEBONE CRICKET CLUB.

WITH

A VIEW OF LORD'S CRICKET GROUND.

"*Even Senators* at cricket urge the ball."—POPE

SECOND EDITION.

LONDON:
ROBERT TYAS, 50, CHEAPSIDE;
J. MENZIES, EDINBURGH.

MDCCCXXXVIII.

See item 34 of the Bibliographical Notes

1844.

LILLYWHITE'S

Illustrated

HAND-BOOK OF CRICKET;

CONTAINING PORTRAITS OF

PILCH.	LILLYWHITE.
BOX.	COBBETT.
A. MYNN, Esq.	G.H.LANGDON, Esq.
C. TAYLOR, Esq.	R. KYNASTON, Esq.

ALSO,

THE LAWS OF CRICKET,

AND OTHER USEFUL INFORMATION

EDITED BY A CANTAB.

Price, with Portrait of Lillywhite, 1s.
With Portraits of Four Players, 2s.
With Portraits of Four Gentlemen, and Four Players, neatly
Bound in Cloth, 3s. 6d.

LONDON:
ACKERMANN & CO., STRAND;
BRIGHTON:
W. H. MASON, REPOSITORY OF ARTS.

See item 45 of the Bibliographical Notes

editions, not all reliable, issued by entrepreneurial publishers. R. S. Rait Kerr's study of the subject published in 1950 is utterly invaluable for those who wish to know more.

One who took great interest in the laws and their application for his particular era was William Denison. Denison, a reporter for several daily newspapers, was of a slightly eccentric bent. He used to dash from ground to ground wearing a wig, a tall wide-brimmed top hat and a long frock-coat. As a young man he had run races with his fellow Parliamentary reporter, Charles Dickens. In April 1844 there appeared Denison's **Cricketer's Companion,** which covered the season 1843 and was the first of six issues treating four seasons' activity. The importance of the Companion lies in its illumination of areas not covered by Haygarth in **Scores and Biographies** and also in the plethora of facts about the players, though these tend to get in the way of individual idiosyncrasies that, if included, would give a more rounded portrait.

In 1846 William Denison produced **Sketches of the Players,** an enduring contemporary review. Among the sketches was one of William Lillywhite, 'the father figure of the famous family', who revolutionized the art of bowling. **Lillywhite's Illustrated Handbook of Cricket** (1844) also contained portraits of illustrious players, in which he shunned false modesty by including himself. The publication of the handbook heralded the beginning of a 55-year association of the Lillywhite dynasty and the bibliographical side of cricket, which will be referred to again later.

Inexcusably, Denison, in two of his Sketches, omitted to give a full monograph of the extraordinary Nicholas Wanostrocht ('Felix' to all but the parents of his pupils), though he was preeningly proud of the fact that he had once captured the great man's wicket. Schoolmaster, musician, artist, inventor and Kent cricketer: there was little, it seemed, to which Felix could not turn his hand successfully; certainly, **Felix on the Bat — being a scientific enquiry into the use of the Cricket Bat together with the History and Use of the Catapulta** (1845) is a treatise of rare charm, humour and craft, enhanced by black and white and also water-colour illustrations from originals by G. F. Watts. There were three editions over a ten-year period, and that is not including much of the body of the book, which Alexander Paterson acknowledges is part of his **Manual of Cricket,** published in New York in 1847. In 1962, the inveterate 'Felix' enthusiast, Gerald Brodribb, provided an excellent memoir of the effervescent Wanostrocht which incorporated a reprint of the second edition of **Felix on the Bat** and then, in 1985, amplified our knowledge with a survey of his work as an artist and author. This was issued as a limited edition of 220 copies.

Manuals in booklet form, containing instructions and guidelines, with historical précis thrown in, were in vogue throughout the middle years of the 19th century. **The Cricketer's Manual by "Bat"** excelled most with its wide-ranging information, layout and originality; it appeared between 1848 and 1851. 'Bat', the pseudonym for Charles Box, a schoolmaster much given to verbose prose, who wrote widely on themes remote from cricket, was many years later to produce two worthy tomes on his favourite sport: **The Theory and Practice of Cricket** and **The English Game of Cricket**. After giving up teaching, Box became a rather aloof cricket editor of 'The Times' and then 'The Field'. Apparently, he mellowed when indulging his liking for port.

We can now discern that from around 1850 the cricket book-buying public proliferated to a marked degree. Following the example of the Nottinghamshire cricketer, William Clarke, many different teams of celebrated players toured the country with greater facility owing to the Industrial Revolution, and they obviously engendered an enthusiasm for information of all kinds. Apart from the publications already mentioned, there were many others jostling for a place on the bookstall: Fred Lillywhite's **Guide** staked an annual claim; Dipple, Banks, Heywood, Bayly, Routledge and Thorp all tested the water and some found it too hot for their aspirations. Ventures were made abroad as well: laws were issued in Toronto, club scores published in Calcutta and annuals marketed in Melbourne. Yet at '2 New Coventry St., Haymarket, W.', in London, a diminutive figure known as the 'Little Wonder' had been busy consolidating his sports accessories business. The House of Wisden was ready to publish its first almanack.

Victorian Tome to Twentieth-Century Treadmill

If John Wisden were alive today, he would no doubt be mildly surprised to find his name synonymous with that of books on cricket. For, as a generalization, it is fair to say that even the most uninterested outsider, or one for whom cricket is total anathema, acknowledges hearing of the almanack while, at the same time, professing ignorance of all else to do with the game or its writings.

Wisden was a first-rate player, accurate bowler, steady batsman and, importantly, an astute businessman. His three-year working partnership with the mercurial Fred Lillywhite had been dissolved in 1858, one year before they went on the first ever tour to Canada and the U.S.A., a tour which Wisden helped set up and which Lillywhite reported. At home, Wisden continued on his own in the cricket equipment shop off Leicester Square, preparing for the day, which came in 1863, when he would finish playing for Sussex. In that year, understandably, his thoughts must have concentrated particularly on ways of augmenting his future income.

The first issue of the almanack in 1864 could be bought for one shilling, a price that was to remain unchanged until well into the 20th century. The compendium suitably fed the enquiring Victorian mind with elliptical information on hugely diverse topics: church festivals, 'Varsity boat races, the rules of knur and spell, relations with China and the trial of King Charles I. Cricket found a place therein and then in the following years took a more prominent place. It was not until 1870 that accounts of matches, enlarging on the record of score statistics and written by W. H. Knight, were introduced (Wisden concentrated on the publishing), and what was to become the 'Cricketer's Bible' took on a vivid character all of its own. The almanack lost impetus after Knight's death in 1879, and even more so after Wisden passed away in 1884; but with the advent of the brothers Pardon in successive editorial roles, destiny was assured.

As has been implied, Wisden's growing ascendancy faced competition in different guises and of different duration — long-term, intermittent and short-lived; shooting stars and stayers that all wanted a part of the action from the expanding County Championships, tours to and from other countries, and personalities on

The Cricketer's Almanack,

FOR THE YEAR 1864.

BEING

Bissextile or Leap Year, and the 28th of the Reign of
HER MAJESTY QUEEN VICTORIA,

CONTAINING

The Laws of Cricket,

AS REVISED BY THE MARYLEBONE CLUB;

THE FIRST APPEARANCE AT LORD'S AND NUMBER OF RUNS OBTAINED BY

MANY CRICKETING CELEBRITIES;

SCORES OF 100 AND UPWARDS, FROM 1850 TO 1863;

EXTRAORDINARY MATCHES;

ALL THE MATCHES PLAYED BETWEEN

THE GENTLEMEN AND PLAYERS,

AND

The All England and United Elevens,

With full and accurate Scores taken from authentic sources;

TOGETHER WITH

The Dates of the University Rowing Matches,

THE WINNERS OF THE

DERBY, OAKS, AND ST. LEGER;

RULES OF

BOWLS, QUOITS, AND KNUR AND SPELL,

AND OTHER INTERESTING INFORMATION.

LONDON:

PUBLISHED AND SOLD BY JOHN WISDEN AND CO.,

AT THEIR

CRICKETING AND BRITISH SPORTS WAREHOUSE,

2, NEW COVENTRY STREET, HAYMARKET, W.

May be had of all respectable Booksellers in the United Kingdom, or forwarded free by the Publisher to any part of Great Britain for 13 Stamps.

1864.   **One Shilling.**

See item 93 of the Bibliographical Notes

the field of play. In retrospect, it is easy to decry the various directories, handbooks, pocket-annuals and other publications, from such names as Wilkinson, Feltham, Bryan, Whittam, Sugg, Key and Leng, for being too derivative and mainly insubstantial, and therefore unimportant historically. Nevertheless, that is not true of all of them and, even if most did splutter to a stop fairly quickly, either through being handicapped with insufficient capital or in suffering the consequences of being too localized, they reflected the growing interest of their time and deserve recognition for that alone. There is no question, however, that the only really serious sustained rivalry to Wisden came from the Lillywhite Companions, and then Annuals, which did not finally concede defeat until the new century had begun.

There were many other noteworthy arrivals to be accommodated on the shelves of book-loving Victorian devotees. The continuing compilations of **Scores and Biographies** by Arthur Haygarth, for instance, the complete run of which any serious student of cricket cannot afford to be without, represent a monumental amount of research that is almost without parallel. Gradually, books of instruction grew fewer and tour reports dominated: R. A. Fitzgerald's **Wickets in the West** (an engrossing narrative of 'The Gentlemen of the MCC' enjoying themselves in America) and the England versus Australia confrontations detailed by such as P. E. Reynolds, C. F. Pardon, S. Billingham, and G. Brumfitt and J. I. Kirby, are examples.

The first organized visit to South Africa by an English side in 1888–89 galvanized two publishers in Port Elizabeth into rapid production, though unfortunately one, Impey Walton, lost most of their stock in a fire: they tried to recoup some of their losses by bringing out an account of the visit by W. W. Read's side three years later. The two tours led by Lord Hawke to the same country, as well as his forays to America and India, all received printed documentation. Similarly, Hawke's team visiting Barbados in 1896–97, alongside the team of Arthur Priestley, spurred an account by A. B. Price which, together with two books that covered R. Slade Lucas's tour of the West Indies two years earlier, make glittering treasure trove for acquisitive collectors. One should not overlook, either, two other early tour accounts that reveal the places and the people with as much certainty as they do the cricket: **Ten thousand miles through India and Burma** (1903), Cecil Headlam's description of the Oxford University Authentics tour, and **With the M.C.C. to New Zealand** (1907) by Percy May, which includes a short history of New Zealand cricket by John F. Macpherson.

The mention of W. W. Read's name just now is a reminder of his own **Annals of Cricket** (1896), which recounted his playing experience over twenty-three years, and it also recalls the record of his performances for Surrey and in representative cricket that was circulated privately in a limited edition in 1897 by the Marquis de Santa Susana. The Marquis (one Anthony Benitez De Lugo) produced two other books on Surrey cricket and all three efforts were printed in Madrid at the press of Ricardo Fé.

The beginnings of what eventually was termed by some 'the golden age of cricket' had many recorders. Among the first of these was the 'Old Buffer' Frederick Gale, who was followed at various times by practitioners A. G. Steel, R. H. Lyttelton, Richard Daft, Ranjitsinghi the 'Indian Prince' and, of course, W. G. himself, with just a little help from his friends. Their good advice and personal reminiscences were generally dispensed in weighty tomes which exuded an aura of dignity that undoubtedly matched their status.

Cricket's professional historians (a loose description), amongst whom were Alfred Gaston, A. D. Taylor and, above all, F. S. Ashley-Cooper, each in their own way made crucial contributions to furthering our knowledge of early cricket and its development. In their specialist area, Gaston and Taylor compiled valuable bibliographies that, even then, between eighty and one hundred years ago, displayed the difficulty in tracing all of the game's writings, whereas Ashley-Cooper, whose lifetime's meticulous research into practically every corridor and cranny of cricket is nothing short of incredible, specialized in every area. If one had to choose one title from over a hundred books and pamphlets with which to illustrate Ashley-Cooper's encyclopaedic approach, it would have to be **Cricket Highways and Byways** (1927), which includes chapters headed 'Winter Cricket', 'A Girdle Round the Earth', 'Charles Dickens and Cricket', 'Cricket and the Church' and 'Books and Writers'. Irving Rosenwater aptly characterized Ashley-Cooper as 'the Herodotus of Cricket'.

As the 20th century unfolded, more books of recollection by distinguished players or, alternatively, dissertations on their careers from others, began to be published: Robert Abel, Stanley Jackson and Sammy Woods are three that come to mind immediately. 'Plum' Warner, eminent on and in cricket fields for nearly seventy years, also wrote prolifically about the game, his *magnum opus*, **Imperial Cricket** (1912), being dedicated by gracious permission to the King Emperor. The vellum-bound volume reflects cricket worldwide (or at least as far as the pink had run on the map, which is virtually the same thing) and it is not surprising, in view of Warner's own aspirations, that the opening chapter is entitled 'Cricket and the Royal Family'.

In 1921, Warner founded and edited 'The Cricketer', which in timely fashion mended the rupture that international conflict had caused in the virtually unbroken line of periodicals, chiefly concerned with the game, that had been published since a paper of the same name made a solitary appearance in December 1869. Predominant for thirty or so years from 1882 was 'Cricket', which ran weekly throughout the season and monthly during autumn and winter, and was edited for most of that time by C. W. Alcock. There were several competitors which petered out, although abroad 'The American Cricketer' led the field unhindered from 1877 to 1929.

By and large, the annuals were no more secure than most periodicals, though a few did manage a lengthy tenure: **Natal Cricketers' Annual** (which later became **South African Cricketers' Annual**) (1884/85–1906/07); **The Barbados Cricketer's Annual** (1894/95–1913/14); **Ayre's Cricket Companion** (1902–31); and, lasting longest with Methuselah-like tenacity, **The Athletic News,** an annual which was born in 1888 and, apart from breaks for the two World Wars, did not expire finally until it was under the aegis of the 'Sunday Chronicle' in the post-war decade from 1946. Those who collect in this area realise that, of all the 20th-century cricket annuals, undoubtedly the hardest to find in its entirety is **John Wisden's Cricketer's Notebook** (1900–13), edited by F. S. Ashley-Cooper and containing much extraordinary notabilia.

There is little sense of chronological order in the cricket books which have been published in the last eighty years, or even in the period before; however, with few memorable exceptions, there is a definite sense of category. Cricket writing had matured by the early 1900s, mirroring Edwardian confidence; literary ability was more widespread; indeed, cricket itself had had time to have a past worth writing about. There was enough now on the shelves to warrant a convenient indexing under type, encompassing such categories as history, biography, tour report, technical treatise, statistical survey and reference guide. The momentum has never slowed, except during the world wars, and there is now so much to put onto the shelves, nearly all of it available in theory and some of it unavailable in reality, that no one person or even library can hope to aim at comprehensiveness; and so to collect a type or category is perhaps the only feasible alternative.

Random examples from a few categories demonstrate the unquestionable ability of a game of bat and ball to stir men's pens:

History: **The Hambledon Men** by E. V. Lucas; **A History of Cricket** by Altham (in later editions, by Altham and Swanton); **Old English Cricket** by 'H. P.-T.' (P. F. Thomas); **Australian Cricket** by A. G. Moyes; and **Cricket, a history** by Rowland Bowen.

Biography: **Seventy-One Not Out,** reminiscences of William Caffyn, edited by 'Mid-On'; **Fred** by John Arlott; **'My Dear Victorious Stod'** (referring to A. E. Stoddart) by David Frith; **Sir Donald Bradman** by Irving Rosenwater; and **C. B., the Life of Charles Burgess Fry** by Clive Ellis.

Technique: **Great Batsmen: their methods at a glance** and **Great Bowlers and Fielders: their methods at a glance,** both by C. B. Fry and George W. Beldham.

Reference: **The Complete Who's Who of Test Cricketers** by Christopher Martin-Jenkins; **Who's Who of Cricketers** by Philip Bailey, Philip Thorn and Peter Wynne-Thomas; and **The Collins Who's Who of English First-Class Cricket** by Robert Brooke.

Tours: **The Book of the two Maurices** by Turnbull and Allom; **Kissing the Rod** by P. G. H. Fender; **The West Indies in Australia: the 1930–31 cricket tour,** edited by 'Old Colour' with the collaboration of The Judge; and **Cricket Walkabout** by D. J. Mulvaney.

Appreciation: **Cricket by Firelight** by Richard Binns; and **Cricket all his Life,** 'collected' by Rupert Hart-Davis.

The modern era of writing on the noble game has been dominated by Neville Cardus and John Arlott. In 1969, they collaborated to produce a book of fine prints, **The Noblest Game,** which contains a reflective view of cricket's historical span from Cardus, and authoritative introductions to 60 beautifully reproduced old prints and paintings from Arlott. For the connoisseur of cricketing art it forms a natural relationship with **The Noble Game of Cricket** (1941), which was composed of superbly illustrated drawings and prints from the Sir Jeremiah Colman collection. Any 'Cardus on cricket' bears witness to the high plateau of prose that is within. To search through **Days in the Sun** (1924), **The Summer Game** (1929), **Cricket** (1930), **Autobiography** (1947), **Second Innings** (1950), **Close of Play** (1956) and **Full Score** (1970), is to discover the essential Neville Cardus. More recently, devotees are in debt to Margaret Hughes, who has gathered together half a dozen collections of Cardus's work.

John Arlott has a unique place in cricket literature. He has an enviable ability to 'bring alive' any incident or situation, and yet place it in perspective with brevity. The Arlottian phrase is unmistakable, and has the advantage of evoking 'The Voice' heard for so many years over the airwaves. A prodigious output on many subjects, including infantile paralysis, topography, wine, cheese and snuff, produced over four decades, makes restricted coverage of even his cricket writing somewhat unrepresentative. It ranges from book journals to reader's guides, from biography to history, and from poetry and anthology to monographs of the players, mostly but not exclusively Hampshire, produced (often as an offprint from a 'County Yearbook') in limited edition.

One of the most important books on the game arrived from the West Indies in 1963. **Beyond a Boundary,** by the scholarly C. I. P. James, is exceptional because it does not confine its philosophy to cricket. It explores in depth the interrelation of the game and racial politics in the Caribbean, and, with the benefit of hindsight, one can see pointers for today and the future for other parts of the cricket world.

Other notable additions that deserve to be charted have come from the novelist A. A. Thomson. A rich vein of humour is apparent in **Cricket My Pleasure** (1953), **Cricket My Happiness** (1954), and **Cricket the Great Captains** (1965). Alan Gibson produced a book with a roughly similar title in 1979, **The Cricket Captains of England,** demonstrating concise construction within a wide vocabulary. In 1933, R. C. Robertson-Glasgow compiled a selection of prose and verse sketches, gleaned mostly from 'The Cricketer', in **The Brighter Side of Cricket;** and over the next 30 years he produced several collections of his own humorous and highly individual newspaper writings and a charming autobiography, **46 not out.** Denzil Batchelor edited and introduced in 1967 some **Best Cricket Stories. The Story of Continental Cricket** by P. C. G. Labouchere, T. A. J. Provis and P. S. Hargreaves made a novel appearance in the bookshops in 1969, the three authors possessing between them greater or lesser mastery of 14 European languages, plus a superficial knowledge of Slavic and Celtic tongues. A cataloguer might be tempted to bracket this offering with **Strangers' Gallery** (1974) by Allen Synge, which looks at some foreign views of English cricket, although there is little similarity. Synge paired with Leo Cooper to unearth accounts of odd games of cricket played in unexpected places, under the title **Tales from Far Pavilions** (1984). J. M. Kilburn said **Thanks to Cricket** in 1972, in a book 'compounded of autobiography, biography, appreciation, history, evaluation, philosophy, sometimes wise, sometimes nostalgic, always traditional and idealistic.' **Fingleton on Cricket** was available in the same year, and so was **Sort of a Cricket Person,** which was more than an autobiography of E. W. Swanton. The book, titled from a remark made by a child, encompassed a range of experience and activity that knew no boundaries. Written in that incomparable conversational style that is distinctly his own, Jim Swanton covers all sides of the media, sports other than cricket, and social life, as well as providing a moving insight into his time as a POW of the Japanese. **Follow On** (1977) is a companion volume containing informed, charming and civilized reminiscences on a variety of topics: Lord's, aspects of Oxford, body-line, and a few 'old buffers'.

As I said at the Time is an impressive modern tome encompassing a lifetime of writing by E. W. S., edited by the Hon. George Plumptre.

Other recent publications include **Cricket Addicts Archive** by Benny Green (who has also edited **A Cricketer's Diary** and four enormous anthologies culled from Wisden as well as compiling a **Book of Obituaries**), **In Celebration of Cricket** by Kenneth Gregory, and **The Joy of Cricket** by John Bright-Holmes. This is surely proof positive that there is still a rich well of untapped material awaiting re-release in anthological form. In **Cricket in Isolation (the Politics of Race and Cricket in South Africa)**, edited and published in Cape Town by André Odendaal, the author sets out 'to record for posterity the wide spectrum of views held by a number of leading personalities, representatives of their respective groups at this historic juncture in time.' **The Packer Affair,** by Henry Blofeld, covers the saga of another fractious episode in cricket. **The Golden Age of Cricket 1890–1914** by David Frith, with a Foreword from J. B. Priestley, has rare photographs, most of them previously unpublished, pleasing colour reproductions from 'Vanity Fair' and Chevalier Taylor, and informative cameos. The whole presentation gives convincing support to the author's contention that 'of all the phases in Cricket's history none has the seductive charm of the late Victorian and Edwardian period.'

And so the writings of cricket multiply year by year: one can barely touch the fringe. There is no room to expand with **England on Tour** by Peter Wynne-Thomas, **Patrons, Players and the Crowd (the Phenomenon of Indian Cricket)** by Richard Cashman, **On Reflection** by Richie Benaud, **Art of Cricket** by Simon and Smart, **The Way to Lord's, Cricketing letters to The Times** by Marcus Williams, and **Game in Season** by J. S. Finch; or to express delight at the work of so many more who venture into print, such as Mike Brearley and Peter Roebuck. Alas, it is mortifying to realise that many gems from even a hundred or so years ago, such as the simple odes of 'Old Stump', Abel Kidd and afterwards the delightfully inconsequential goings-on related in J. M. Barrie's two minuscule **Allahakbarrie** books, are uncherished on these pages.

It is salutary to quote John Arlott from his resumé of cricket literature in the 1963 **Wisden**: 'Cricket writing has grown up side by side with Wisden. In 1864 a small, but growing, number of writers and publishers were searching for acceptable methods of presenting the game. Now . . .virtually every possible style and formula has been used.'

As has been seen, not all from Victoria's time was weighty and portentous; neither is everything written today a product of the publishing treadmill, capitalizing on the response and interest of the public generated by the limited-over 'thrash'. Quite the reverse is apparent in so many cases. In the last few years, explorations into the pictorial history of cricket, and also massive excavations to unearth the biographical and career data of every player who has taken part in a first-class game, have been undertaken and successfully accomplished.

When E. W. (Tim) Padwick finally presented **A Bibliography of Cricket** in its first edition in 1977, the culmination of a corporate effort launched nearly thirty years earlier, his relief and elation at off-loading at last an unequalled and exhausting undertaking must have been matched by feelings of utter frustration. He was only too aware that an escalating list of further titles was running away even before he could draw breath. The only consolation, perhaps, was to climb a metaphysical plane, as did 'Dwarpa' in 'Cricket as allied to the Heavens', or to come down to earth with **Certain Personal Matters** by H. G. Wells. The 'Veteran Cricketer' was 'seized', he says, 'some scores of years ago now, by sciatica, clutched indeed about the loins thereby, and forcibly withdrawn from the practice of the art; since when a certain predisposition to a corpulent habit has lacked its natural check of exercise, and a broadness almost Dutch has won upon him.' When, as sometimes happens, that day finally arrives, we may at least still try to emulate Blunden's friendly poet:

Have you not ever felt the urge to write
Of all the cricket that has blessed your sight?

Eighth

MUSÆ
JUVENILES.

Per *Gulielmum Goldwin*, A. B.
Collegii Regalis Socium.

———— *Studiis florentem ignobilis oti,*
Carmina quæ lusi. —— Virg. Georgic. Lib. 4.

LONDINI,

Proſtant Venales apud *A. Baldwin,* in Vico
Vulgo dcto *Warwick-lane,* 1706.

See item 1

BIBLIOGRAPHICAL NOTES ON
EARLY BOOKS

1. **In certamen pilae.** *Musae Juveniles per Gulielmum Goldwin A. B.
    Collegii Regalis Socium. A. Baldwin, Warwick Lane, March 1706.*
    4pp. This is the earliest description of a match in Latin verse. A
    translation by Harold Perry was published in 'Etoniana' No. 31, in
    Dec. 1922. H. P.-T. (P. F. Thomas), in **More Old Cricket** (1926),
    understood that a biography of Goldwin by the Rev. Dr Orford,
    privately circulated in 1911, contained a translation of 'In certamen
    pilae'. Thomas gives his own translation in **Early Cricket** (1923).
    William Goldwin was a native of Windsor, who, for the last thirty
    years of his life, served as vicar of St. Nicholas's, Bristol.

2. **Cricket: an heroic poem.** *Illustrated with the critical observations
    of Scriblerus Maximus* [James Dance]. *Printed for W. Bickerton, in
    the Temple Exchange, near the Inner Temple Gate, Fleet St., 1744.*
    25pp. Dance's real name was Love. Some mildly satirical lines in
    his poem about the Artillery Ground caused offence to the Hon.
    Company and he was threatened with prosecution. However, the
    matter was dropped. There were five editions in Love's lifetime and
    a sixth in 1922 on the bicentenary of his birth.

3. **The Game at Cricket, As settled by the Several Cricket Clubs,
    Particularly that of the Star and Garter In Pall-Mall.** *Printed for
    M. Read and sold by W. Reeve in Fleet Street. 1755.* 19pp. This is
    the first known publication of the Laws in booklet form. P. F.
    Thomas, in **Old-Time Cricket,** mentions that an issue of the Laws
    emanated in the same year from Robert Sayer at the Golden Buck,
    Fleet Street, but this is thought to be a mistake. An earlier manuscript
    of Laws is now lost, though the Duke of Richmond/A. Brodrick
    Articles of agreement (1727) exist, as do linen handkerchiefs with
    printed laws from Joseph Ware of Crayford and a different version
    once in the possession of W. J. Humphry.
    A number of reliable and also unreliable pamphlets and broad-
    sheets came out in the eighteenth century: those by Ridley, Clout,

SURRY TRIUMPHANT:

OR THE

Kentiſh - Mens Defeat.

A NEW BALLAD;

BEING

A   P A R O D Y

O N

C H E V Y - C H A C E.

————*Viciſti, et victum tendere* nummos
Cantiaci *vidére*————   VIRG. ÆN. xii. variat.
And ſwift flew the cricket-ball over the lawn.

ANON.

L O N D O N:

Printed for J. JOHNSON, No. 72, in St. Paul's Church-yard.

1773.

See item 4

THE

KENTISH CRICKETERS:

A   POEM.

By a GENTLEMAN.

BEING

A REPLY to a late Publication of a PARODY
on the Ballad of CHEVY CHACE ;

INTITULED,

SURRY TRIUMPHANT:

OR, THE

KENTISH MEN's DEFEAT.

Justitiæ partes sunt non violare homines : Verecundiæ non offendere.   TULL.

Justice consists in doing no Injury to Men: Decency in giving them no Offence.

CANTERBURY: Printed by T. SMITH and SON :
And sold by THEM, and W. FLACKTON : Also, by B. LAW, in
Avemary-lane ; Messrs. RICHARDSON and URQUHART, under the
Royal Exchange, LONDON ; and all other BOOKSELLERS.

1 7 7 3.

See item 5

Williams, Reynell, Wallis, Blake and Turpin are but some. R. S. Rait Kerr's **The Laws of Cricket** (1950) has a nearly comprehensive listing.

4. **Surry Triumphant: or the Kentish-mens defeat;** *a new ballad; being a parody on the Chevy-Chace.* [John Duncombe.] *Printed for J. Johnson, 1773. No. 72 in St. Paul's Churchyard.* 24pp. A match is described that was played at the Bishopsbourne Paddock seat of Sir Horatio Mann. It is a very clever exercise, as about half the words in most of the 66 verses are the same as in the original Chevy-Chace ballad. The Rev. John Duncombe, M.A., was curate of Sundridge, near Sevenoaks.

5. **The Kentish Cricketers:** *a poem. By a gentleman. Being a reply to a late publication of a parody on the Ballad of Chevy Chase; intituled Surry triumphant; or, The Kentish Men's defeat.* [John Burnby.] *Printed by T. Smith & Son, and sold by them and W. Flacton; also, by B. Law, in Avemory Lane; Messrs. Richardson and Urquhart, under the Royal Exchange, 1773.* 22pp. This is an inter-county retort, again in verse, by an attorney-at-law.

6. **The Noble Cricketers:** *a poetical and familiar epistle, address'd to two of the idlest Lords in his Majesty's Three Kingdoms. J. Bew, 1778.* 22pp. The poem mounts a scathing attack on the Duke of Dorset and the Earl of Tankerville, principally for their devoting so much time to cricket 'whilst Britain for her slaughter'd Legions sighs.'

7. **The cryketeers:** *Williams* [of Wadham College]. *The blunders of loyalty, and other miscellaneous poems; being a selection of certain ancient poems, partly on subjects of local history. Together with the original notes and illustrations, etc. The poems modernized by Ferdinando Fungus, Gent. Printed for J. Murray. 1790.* 2pp. 'The cryketeers' is facetiously described as a 'gymnastic poeme' by Edmunde Byrk.

8. **A Sketch-book.** *George Shepheard.* [c.1790.] Shepheard's Sketch-book is kept at Lord's. The page depicting typical poses by Beauclerk, Beldham, Bligh, Cumberland, Harris, Lennox, Lord, Tufton, Walker, Shepheard himself and presumably one other has been reproduced in several volumes, notably as a frontispiece to E. V. Lucas's **The Hambledon Men** (1907) and as a plate in **The Noblest Game** by Cardus and Arlott (1969).

T H E

ṄOBLE CRICKETERS:

A POETICAL AND FAMILIAR

E   P   I   S   T   L   E,

A D D R E S S ' D   T O

TWO OF THE IDLEST LORDS

I N H I S M A J E S T Y's

T H R E E   K I N G D O M S.

Ovo prognatus eadem.

L O N D O N Printed:

SOLD BY J: BEW, NO. 28, PATERNOSTER ROW, 1778.

[P R I C E O N E S H I L L I N G.]

See item 6

[27]

The CRYKETEERS.

*A gymnaſtic Pocme, ſublyme and beautiful, in the modern
Faſhyon, and wrytten in four-and-twenty Cantos by my
eſtemed Friende* EDMUNDE BYRK, *Eſqúyr.*

WHILES other bard Coxcombo's folly ſings,
　　To meaner themes attune the lyre,
I in wild phrenſy ſweep th' *infeĉtious* ſtrings,
　My *vocal* ſingers muſic, and my *numbers fire!*
　　　　I ſing of cricket,
　　　　　And the *martial* wicket,
The *ruffian* bat, and leathern-coated ball.
When gentle Zephyr has *drank up* the equinoxial rains, ⎤
Refreſh'd by *ſcalding ſuns*, the *verdant* ſwains, ⎥
By troops aſſembling on the mantling plains, ⎦
　　　　All, all,
　　　　Fly for the ball,
　　And higglety pigglety on it fall!

As ſome lone, thirſty tyger, *weeping* for his mate,
　On ſea beach prowling, whiles the *whiſtling* ſtorm
Stirs up his fury and provokes his fate,
　Not chains of adamant confine his rage forlorn!
Speechleſs for grief——his howling dolorous the diſmal tale
　relates,
And eke betrays the famine ſore, the which his love creates.
　　　　D 2　　　　　　　　　So

A poem modernized by Ferdinando Fungus, Gent. See item 7.

28   T<small>HE</small> CRYKETEERS.

So the *fierce* Cricketeer, with bat of beechen tree,
Strikes the terrific ball——the plain refounds
With trilling clangors !—— * * * *

Cætera defunt.

E<small>DITOR</small>. *Hiatus eheu valdè deflendus!* The obfcure fublimity and afto-
nifhing bathos in this beautiful little fragment, induced the Editor to give it a
place amongft thefe ancient poems, which the Reader will not be forry for—But
the lofs the world has fuftained in the defalcation of twenty-four cantos, equally
terrible and pathetic, cannot eafily be eftimated.-——In part of a note by that
indefatigable old commentator and faithful hiftorian Sir Mar-truth Puzzle-pate
Gibbon, which has efcaped the general ruin of this poem, it appears that the
writer was a man of great literary fame in the time of our author, and as much
celebrated for the prolixity of his oratorical effufions, as for his poetical; having
been known to hold forth for ten hours without intermiffion. " In thefe his fits of
" oratorie," fays one, " he didd not refufe nouryfhment while as occafion didd
" ferve ; but didd neither hymfelf take, nor permit to any other, a found nap,
" altho' it be he didd many tymes *doze and dream*, as I haue heard faye ; Horace
" having not denied that leave—*op· è in longo fas eft oppreffere fomnum*—but hys
" patient auditors didd freely ufe thys pryviledge here by the poet in thys cafe
" made and provyded."

T H E

53

L I S T

OF ALL THE

PRINCIPAL MATCHES.

OF

C R I C K E T,

That have been played in the Year 1790;

WITH

A CORRECT STATE OF EACH INNINGS.

BY

SAMUEL BRITCHER, Scorer.

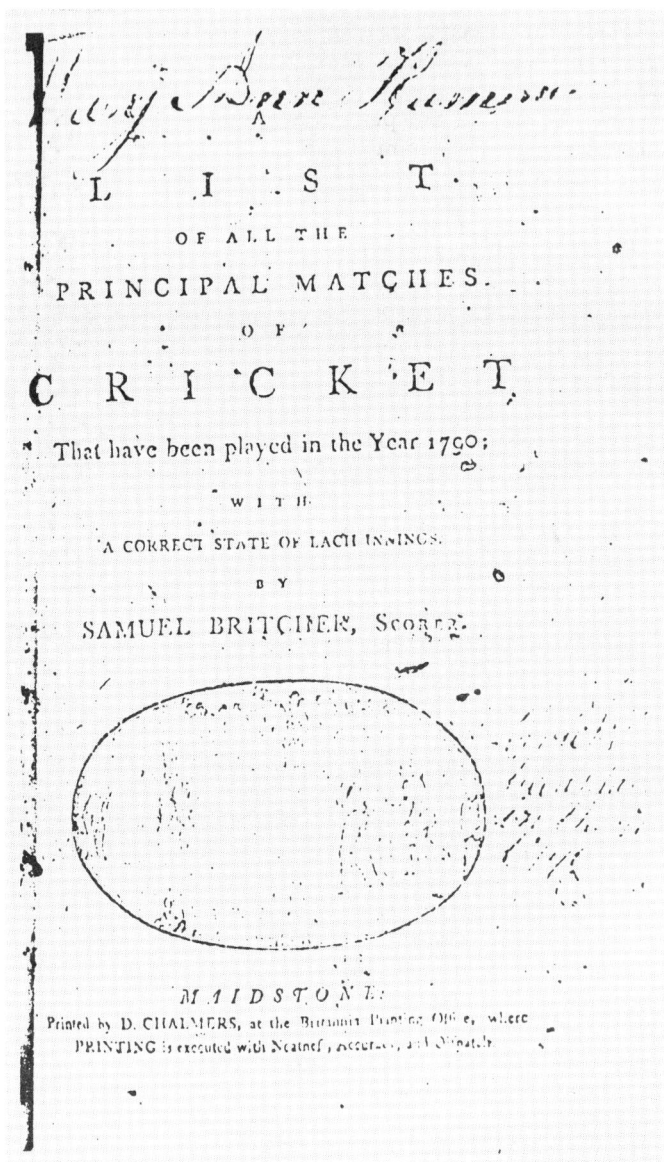

MAIDSTONE:

Printed by D. CHALMERS, at the Britannia Printing Office, where
PRINTING is executed with Neatness, Accuracy, and Dispatch.

See item 9

9. **List of all the principal matches of cricket that have been played in the year.** [1790–1805.] *With a correct state of each innings. Samuel Britcher.* The first cricket annual by the M.C.C. scorer had various paginations and publishers for the 15 issues. (For a full guide, see the booklet **Samuel Britcher: the hidden scorer.**) Stanhope and Graham compiled the last two years in one volume.

10. **Cricket: a collection of all the grand matches of cricket, played in England, within twenty years;** *viz. from 1771 to 1791, never before published. W. Epps. Arranged and printed by W. Epps, Troy-town, Rochester. 1799.* 104pp. Epps informs that the scores are 'carefully corrected from the collections of several Gentlemen, none of which have ever been published.'

11. **Rules and Instructions for Playing at the Game of Cricket** *as practised by the most eminent players; to which is subjoined the laws and regulations of cricketters* [sic] *as revised by the Cricket Club at Mary-le-Bone. Thomas Boxall. Printed by Harrild and Billing.* [c.1801.] 92pp. There were three editions between 1801 and 1804. In Padwick's **A Bibliography of Cricket** (1977 and 1984) are listed two issues of the second edition and three issues of the third, all with minor typographical variations. However, the 1981 reprint of Boxall, with an introduction and appendices by Diana Rait Kerr, credits the second edition with three issues.

12. **The original and unrivalled Mosslake Field Cricket Society:** *we the undersigned having become members of this Society do hereby agree to stand to and observe the following* **rules and regulations.** *Mosslake Field Cricket Society, 1807.* Broadsheet. Mosslake Field C.S. later became Liverpool C.C., who once humbled mighty Yorkshire. (**Matches of the Liverpool Cricket Club, 1847–64** was printed in 1865.) Also in existence is a morocco-backed 160-page manuscript scorebook of Liverpool C.C. for 1822/23. It includes a game against an 'All-England' team.

13. **Boston Cricket Club.** *Members only. Boston, 1809.* There is very little information to hand. Alfred D. Taylor, in his **Catalogue of Cricket Literature** (1906), comments, 'of value on account of its antiquity but of no real interest.' Presumably, **Laws of Cricket** (Boston, 1806) was issued from the same area, which is likely to be the American city and not the Lincolnshire town.

14. **Bramshill Cricket Club.** *1810.* Little information has been available about this publication. The item appears in Appendix II addenda of Taylor, and J. W. Goldman, in his **Bibliography of Cricket** (1937), remarks, 'Very scarce — a collector's item, solely.'

15. **Established rules of the Goodwood Cricket Club,** *July 5, 1813. Chichester, 1813. Printed by William Mason.* 8pp. Only one copy has come to light and it is held at the West Sussex Record Office in Chichester.

16. **Garrison Cricket Club.** *4 August 1816.* 2pp. This item is unique and precious. Membership before the 15th of the month was 5 francs and thereafter 10 francs. E. W. A. Hay was secretary and treasurer and Sir Thomas Brisbane was to be 'solicited to accept the office of President . . . The Game played on the Plain of Mons. The Committee will meet every Thursday at Wright's Hotel, Rue de Grand Fossart. Dress in white jacket and trousers. No member can leave the Game without the unanimous consent of the parties playing and in such case a substitute will be required of the retiring member.'

17. **Instructions and rules for playing the noble game of cricket,** *as practised by the most eminent players: containing a variety of directions little known to players in general . . . Illustrated by an Elegant Copper-Plate Engraving, Exhibiting the Players in the Field . . . To which are subjoined The Laws of the Game with additions and corrections — by William Lambert. Sussex Press, Lewes. Printed and Published by J. Baxter, and sold in London by Baldwin and Co. Paternoster Row, and all Booksellers. 1816.* 55pp. The puzzle surrounding the numbering of the editions is unlikely ever to be solved. There are 13 known editions, the penultimate being numbered 20th and the last, which was published circa 1830–32, being numbered 12th. The 13th–19th editions have not been found and were probably never produced. One could speculate that the missing editions were burned by Lambert's relatives, some of whom were found to be using copies of the book to light the fire, though it is highly improbable that others would not have survived elsewhere.

     A few of the editions had more than one issue, containing minor differences and more than one year's watermark. It is almost possible to build a case for 19 different issues from these disparate elements by the time that the 20th edition actually arrived, but not quite. In any case, it is a far from feasible theory.

ESTABLISHED

RULES

OF THE

GOODWOOD

CRICKET CLUB;

JULY 5, 1813.

Chichester:

PRINTED BY WILLIAM MASON,

1813.

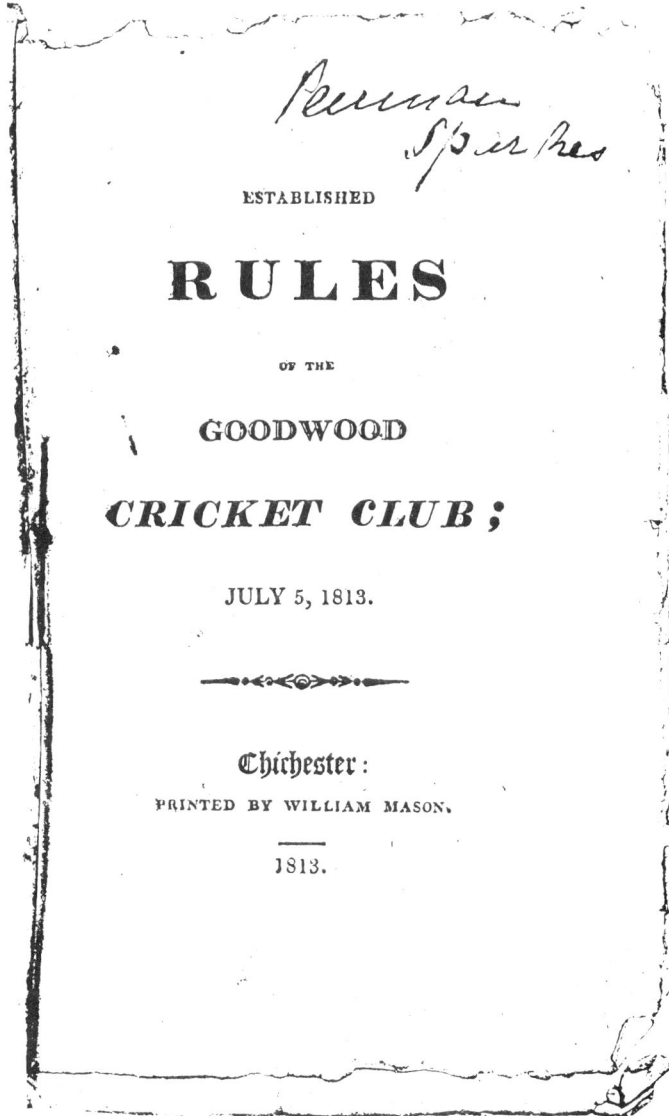

See item 15. *West Sussex Record Office, Goodwood Ms. 1887. Reproduced by courtesy of the Directors of the Goodwood Estate Company Limited and with acknowledgements to the West Sussex Record Office and the County Archivist.*

Valenciennes 4th. *August* 1816.

AT a meeting of Officers of different Corps, held this day for the purpose of forming a Garrison Cricket Club; it was resolved,

1st.   That Major General Sir Thomas Brisbane, be solicited to accept the office of President.

2nd.   There shall be a regulating Committee, composed of one Member from each Corps and Department, to which the Members forming the Club may belong.

3rd.   The Subscription upon admission of a Member to the Club, before the 15th. of the present Month, shall be 5 Francs, and after that period 10 Francs. Officers of the Division who may not join their Corps until after the 15th. of this Month, will be only required to pay the original Subscription.

4th.   The Game will be played upon the Plain of Mons.

5th.   The Committee will meet every Thursday at Wright's Hotel, *Rue du Grand Fossart*, at one in the afternoon, for the purpose of transacting all business respecting the Club.

6th.   A Marquee will be provided by the Committee, for the exclusive use of the Club, and pitched on all match days at 10 and the Wickets at 11 in the forenoon precisely.
        Refreshments will be provided for the Club, by Mr. Wright at fixed prices.

7th.   There will be two Match days (weather permitting) in every week : at one or other of these days, each Member will de expected to attend.

8th.   The dress of the Club, shall be white Jacket and Trowsers, with which it is requested, that each playing Member will provide himself before the 15th. of this Month.

9th.   No Member can leave the Game, without the unanimous consent of the parties playing, and in such case a substitute will be required of the retiring Member.

10th.   Any Bat, Ball, Stumps or Bails, lost or injured out of fair Play, must be paid for previously to the following meeting of the Club, with the fine of two Francs in addition to the original Cost of each article.

See item 16

It is more likely that Baxter was adopting a promotional gimmick by calling the edition numbered 20th 'England's Standard' and then, when the final edition was issued (the so-called 12th), went back to the original numbering sequence, perhaps, for some reason, regarding 'England's Standard' as a special separate entity.

He had certainly not been slow in promoting the work early on, as can be seen in a circular letter from his proof book:

Sir,

You will particularly be obliging by obtaining, among the Cricketers in your Neighbourhood, as many Subscribers as possible to the annexed Work, for 1817. A liberal allowance will be made for the trouble you may be at. As soon as the number is obtained an order will oblige,

Sir, Your Obedient Servant,

J. Baxter.

Sussex Press, Lewes,

April, 1817.

P.S. Should it not be convenient for you to obtain, as above, you will oblige by handing it over to some other active person. The postage and carriage will be deducted from the amount of the order.

N.B. Should it be more convenient to get the Books from London, it will be easily accomplished by applying to any Bookseller in your Neighbourhood. Many players have adopted the plan of playing for Eleven Books; by paying 1s. each, and the Eleven winning, are entitled to a Book each.

Detailed critical analyses of Lambert's **Cricketer's Guide** are to be found in **The Cricketer** spring annuals of 1942 and 1949. The first is by G. B. Buckley and the second by Colonel R. S. Rait-Kerr. Rait-Kerr's study corrects some inaccuracies in Buckley's; even so, it is wise to refer to both before drawing conclusions.

18. **The Cricketer's Pocket Companion;** *or, Field-Sportsman's Guide: Containing a brief, but at the same time, a comprehensive digest of the Laws, Rules and Regulations, Laid down and practised by the most Scientific Players. Respectfully dedicated to the Members of the Cricket Clubs of the United Kingdom. By a Batsman. London: Printed for J. Bysh, 52, Paternoster Row; and sold by C. Penny, Wood Street, and all booksellers. 1818.* 64pp. This would appear to

A

CORRECT ACCOUNT

OF ALL THE

CRICKET MATCHES

WHICH HAVE BEEN PLAYED

BY THE

Mary=le=bone Club,

AND ALL OTHER

PRINCIPAL MATCHES,

From the Year 1786 to 1822 inclusive.

INSCRIBED

By permission, with the greatest respect,

TO THE NOBLEMEN AND GENTLEMEN, MEMBERS

OF THE

Mary=le=bone Cricket Club,

BY

THEIR DEVOTED AND OBLIGED HUMBLE SERVANT,

HENRY BENTLEY.

LONDON:

Printed by T. TRAVELLER, 43, Park Street, New Road.

1823.

See item 20

be the first edition, in the absence of contrary evidence. The imprint cited above is that on the title page, while the imprint on the printed wrapper is 'Printed by and for Hodgson & Co., 10, Newgate Street', with no date but giving the price as sixpence.

J. W. McKenzie, the well-known bookseller, to whom I am indebted for drawing attention to this unique item, points out that it is not listed in Padwick's **Bibliography**; nor is it listed anywhere else as far as can be discovered.

19. **The Cricketer's Pocket Companion** *or Field-Sportsman's Guide containing a brief but, at the same time, a comprehensive Digest of the Laws, Rules and Regulations laid down and practised by the most scientific Players and Respectfully dedicated to the Members of the Cricket Clubs of the United Kingdom by a batsman. London, 1826. Printed for William Cole, No. 10, Newgate St.* xi + 60 numbered pp. This again is an exceedingly rare item. Lord's, which has a copy of almost all the early books on cricket, does not possess a Cole. As suggested by the title of the work and by the address of the publisher, Cole is almost certainly a subsequent edition of the preceding item.

20. **A Correct Account of all the Cricket Matches which have been played by the Marylebone Club and all other Principal Matches for the year 1786 to 1822 inclusive.** *Inscribed by permission, with the greatest respect, to the Noblemen and Gentlemen, members of the Marylebone Cricket Club by their devoted and obliged humble servant, Henry Bentley. London, 1823. Printed by T. Traveller, 43 Park St., New Road.* 374pp.

An Account of the Principal Cricket Matches, played in the year 1823, *with the particulars of each innings. Published by H. Bentley, 12, Grove St., Lisson Grove. London, 1823. Printed by T. Traveller, 43 Park St., New Road.* 20pp.

A Correct Account of all the Cricket Matches which have been played by the Marylebone Club, and all other Principal Matches in the Years 1824 and 1825, *being an appendix To the book printed in 1823, containing all the principal Matches played from the Year 1786 to the Year 1823 inclusive, which, as also the present Appendix, may be had of H. Bentley, 12 Grove St., Lisson Grove. London, 1826. Printed by T. Traveller, 43 Park St., Dorset Square.* 42pp.

The last supplement was priced at three shillings, and was no doubt considered expensive enough at the time. A recent purchaser of a Bentley minus both supplements forked out about two thousand times as much at auction.

21. **Rules of the Old Westminster Cricket Club.** *Westminster, the Club, 1828. Printed by G. Hayden, Little College St., Westminster.* 4pp. The year 1828 saw the foundation of this club. Sir John Osborn Bt. was chairman.

22. It may be of interest to note a manuscript scorebook of the Magdalen C.C., 1827–29, compiled by F. B. Wright (Oxford) and held at Lord's; also the Stockport C.C. manuscript Minutes for 1837–38, the four-page printed **Rules of the Andover Cricket Club** (no date) and the **Rules of the Beckhampton Cricket Club** (and list of members), which again consists of four pages and was printed in Devizes in about 1820. Lord's also stores a manuscript scorebook of 1832–33 made by William Davies, the scorer for the Brighton Cricket Club (subsequently, a printed book of matches of Brighton C.C., covering the seasons 1849 and 1850, was produced) and a minute book from the Canary Islands with the title **Regulations of the Cricket Club, Port Oratova, Tenerife 1826–28,** which includes a *Soneto* in Spanish.

23. **A Correct Account of all the Cricket Matches played by the Nottingham Old Cricket Club, from 1771 to 1829 inclusive.** *Compiled by W. North. Nottingham, 1830. Printed by R. Sutton, Review Office, Bridlesmith-Gate.* 53pp. A 21-page addendum, covering the years to 1835, was printed by J. Hicklin & Co. at the Journal Office, Nottingham in 1836 (Ashley-Cooper states that there are 19 pages, so he is possibly referring to a separate issue) and a further 28 pages, covering matches up to 1837, also exist. North was a schoolmaster who, at the age of 31, changed his profession to that of Inspector of Corn Returns.

24. **Kingscote Cricket Club.** Taylor states that the handbook was issued annually from 1826 to 1830, and that 'the above books on the famous Old Kingscote Club are very rare and difficult to obtain.' Padwick gives the years as 1825–30.

There is a single copy of a vellum-bound handwritten book of scores for the Club for 1822 which, together with a privately published memoir and autobiographical notes of Henry Robert Kingscote, sold for a relatively low price of £40 at the recent Phillips auction of A. E. Winder's collection.

25. **A short account of the origin of the Kilkenny Cricket Club, and of its proceedings, in the years 1830–1831.** *London, 1832. Printed by Poulter, Gt. Chesterfield St.* 22pp. This book, which has been variously ascribed to Lord Ormonde or Lord Ossory, contains three chapters detailing two games against Ballinasloe and 'a paeon of triumphal rhymes'. In 1832, Kilkenny C.C. boasted a membership of 34 with a nucleus of honorary members drawn from the officers of the Regiments quartered in the county and city.

26. **The Young Cricketer's Tutor;** *comprising full directions for playing the elegant and manly game of Cricket; with a complete version of its laws and regulations: by John Nyren, a player in the celebrated Old Hambledon Club, and in the Marylebone Club. To which is added,* **"The Cricketers of My Time"**, *or Recollections of the most famous Old Players, by the same author. The whole collected and edited by Charles Cowden Clarke. London, 1833. Published by Effingham Wilson, Royal Exchange. Printed by Maurice & Co., Fenchurch St.* 126pp. There have been 11 editions, with variants, and seven modern reprints in a number of forms. The second edition, published in Edinburgh, is the scarcest.

27. **The Cricketer's Register for 1833.** *No. XXVIII — Vol. V* 32pp. The Register for 1833 was published in a series of monthly instalments covering the whole season from April to September. It contains compressed information about many minor and also some major matches.

28. **The principles of scientific batting,** *or Plain rules, founded on the practice of the first professors and amateurs, for the noble game of cricket, by a Gentleman; revised by J. H. Dark* (James Pycroft). *H. Slatter, Oxford, 1835.* 44pp. This was Pycroft's first offering on cricket. There was a new edition in 1844 containing the revised laws of cricket, and a further one the following year. Both ran to 48 pages.

29. **The Pump:** ane righte lamentable dirge composit be Bailzie Peakodde, poet laureate to ye Cricket Club; rendered into modern verse by Dr. Minch. Glasgow, 1835. 8pp. A limited edition of 23 copies

This print faces the title page of Nyren's *Young Cricketer's Tutor*: see item 26.

THE
PRINCIPLES

OF

SCIENTIFIC BATTING;

OR

PLAIN RULES,

𝕱ounded on the 𝕻ractice of the first 𝕻rofessors and 𝕬mateurs,

FOR THE

NOBLE GAME OF CRICKET:

BY

A GENTLEMAN.

REVISED BY J. H. DARK.

A NEW EDITION,

CONTAINING

THE LAWS OF CRICKET,

As Altered and Revised by the Marylebone Club, June 2, 1845.

OXFORD,
H. SLATTER, HIGH STREET:

WHITTAKER AND CO., LONDON ; AND J. H. DARK,
LORD'S CRICKET GROUND.

1s. 6d.

See item 28

was produced of this period dirge, which consists of comic verses relating to Glasgow Cricket Club, describing a game on Glasgow Green.

Incidentally, the scores of Glasgow C.C.'s games against Lanarkshire in the same year, 1835, are a feature of the handwritten diary of cricketer George Quentin, which is in the possession of the present writer. There exists also an undated Glasgow broadsheet (once owned by J. W. Goldman) forbidding the playing of cricket on turnpike roads.

30. **Familiar Instructions for playing the noble Game of Cricket** *according to the Rules and Regulations practised by the most scientific players of this delightful and healthy exercise: with The Laws of the Game to which is added A Treatise on the Art of Running. By an Amateur. London, 1836. Printed and Published by J. Limbird, 143 Strand (near Somerset House).* 40pp. In his Introduction the anonymous amateur makes an unconvincing comparison between cricket and the Persian game of chugan. A further issue of this technical treatise was brought out at a later date by Henry Lea, which ran to 32 pages.

31. **The Cricketer's Guide:** *containing complete instructions to persons of all ages for playing at this healthful and manly exercise and for the choice of the Bat, Ball, and Wickets. With the Laws of the Game by a member of the Marylebone Club. London, Dean and Co. Threadneedle St.* [c. 1836.] 62pp. Dean's name is linked with that of Munday for a second edition, of 1840, which was issued in cloth and paper covers. The booklet includes general observations and hints for playing the game with two, three, four, five, six or seven or more persons.

32. **A correct account of all the cricket matches played by the Ripon Cricket Club, 1813–36,** *compiled by George Gatenby. Ripon 1837. Printed by T. Proctor, Market-Place.* 36pp. Two copies are in the M.C.C. Library at Lord's. There is certainly one other copy extant (it was once in the Winder collection), and possibly more.

33. **Instructions for playing the game of cricket;** *with revised laws as adopted by the principal clubs in The Kingdom.* [c. 1838.] 16pp. Another anonymous offering, it is prefaced with a seven-line paeon to cricket.

34. **The Cricketer's Hand-Book** *containing the origin of the game, remarks on recent alterations, directions for bowling, striking, and placing the players, and the laws as altered by the Marylebone Cricket Club. With a view of Lord's Cricket Ground. 1838. London: Robert Tyas, 50 Cheapside. J. Menzies, Edinburgh. Clarke, Printers, Silver St., Falcon Sq., London.* 37pp. A stylish addition to the title page is a quotation from Pope: 'Even Senators at cricket urge the ball'. In 1838, the same year as the Hand-Book was first published, a second edition was issued with two pages of advertisements, for popular works on flowers and trees, at the back of the book. In 1841, a new edition was produced, but this time only Tyas's name appears on the title page — that of Menzies is absent — at a new address, 8 Paternoster Row. It runs to 48 pages, added to which are eight pages of advertisements. Padwick's **Bibliography** does not mention the second edition.

An American edition was published in 1844 by Saxton, Pierce and Co. at No. 133, 1–2 Washington Street, Boston, and Saxton and Miles in New York. Printed by George Coolidge, at 57 Washington Street, it also contained 48 pages.

35. **Rules and Regulations of the Mexican Union Cricket Club** *revised and corrected by the Committee appointed for that purpose by the subscribers at a General Meeting held in February, 1839* [sic]. *Francis Leeson Ball, Esqr. President; Francis Morphy, Esqr. Vice President; A. Melville, Esqr. Treasurer; Richard Geaves, Esqr. Secretary. Together with the Laws of the Game. Mexico, 1838. Ignacio Cumplido, Printer.* 18pp. British expatriates find a homely corner in a foreign field. The publication includes General Laws, Laws of the game, single wicket and bets. The anniversary dinner and meeting of the club were held in February 1838, when it was resolved to draw up new regulations. By October, the regulations had been finalized, and it was proposed that they be 'printed at the expense of the Club and that each member be furnished with a copy.'

36. **Wykehamical Scores from the year 1825.** [Allen Cowburn.] *Winchester. Robbins and Wheeler. 1838.* 80pp. There were five subsequent editions, the last being produced in 1851. Soon after that date, a privately printed compilation was issued of **The Cricket Matches between Harrow and Eton and Harrow and Winchester from 1818–1852.**

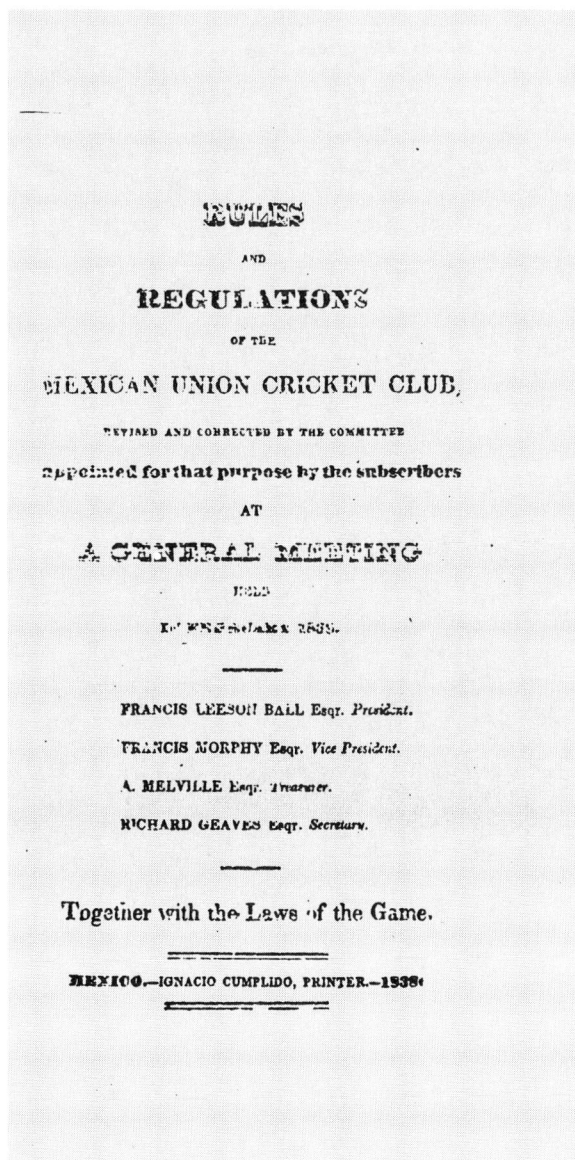

RULES

AND

REGULATIONS

OF THE

MEXICAN UNION CRICKET CLUB,

REVISED AND CORRECTED BY THE COMMITTEE

appointed for that purpose by the subscribers

AT

A GENERAL MEETING

HELD

IN ＊＊＊＊＊＊＊＊ 1838.

FRANCIS LEESON BALL Esqr. *President.*

FRANCIS MORPHY Esqr. *Vice President.*

A. MELVILLE Esqr. *Treasurer.*

RICHARD GEAVES Esqr. *Secretary.*

Together with the Laws of the Game.

MEXICO.—IGNACIO CUMPLIDO, PRINTER.—1838.

See item 35

THE WHOLE ART OF

CRICKET,

AND HOW TO PLAY IT.

INCLUDING

BATTING, BOWLING, FIELDING,

WICKET KEEPING,

LAWS OF DOUBLE WICKET:

WITH INSTRUCTIONS AND GENERAL REMARKS

ON THE GAME.

RULES FOR FORMING A CRICKET CLUB,

AND

LAWS OF SINGLE WICKET.

LONDON:
BISHOP & Co., 101, HOUNDSDITCH.
Price One Penny.

See item 39

37. **Rules and regulations of the Isle of Wight Cricket Club.** *Yelf &*
Co., Newport, Isle of Wight. 1839. This item is mentioned in J. W.
Goldman's **Bibliography of Cricket** (1937).

38. **Rules and regulations of the Harlequin Cricket Club.** *Ryde, Isle*
of Wight. The Club. The Harlequin Cricket Club was formed in
1837. The undated copy of these Rules held in the M.C.C. Library
at Lord's has several manuscript additions.

39. **The Whole Art of Cricket and how to play it;** *including batting,*
bowling, fielding, wicket-keeping; laws of double wicket: with instruc-
tions and general remarks on the game. Rules for Forming a Cricket
Club, and laws of Single Wicket. London. [c. 1840.] *Bishop & Co.,*
101, Houndsditch. Price One Penny. An attractive F. M. Wood
drawing of children playing near a leafy tree, with a windmill in the
background, highlights the title page.

40. **The scores of the Cricket matches played by Rugby School from**
the year MDCCCXXXI. *J. S. Crossley. Rugby, 1842.* 69pp. The
book includes a match against the M.C.C. that is described in **Tom**
Brown's Schooldays. Three further editions followed, in 1852, 1859
and 1864, covering, in all, matches from 1845 to 1864. Crossley's
name is coupled with that of Billington for these editions.

41. **Practical Hints on Cricket, for the direction and guidance of**
beginners, *by a Wykehamist* [Frederick Gale]. *Davies, Cheltenham,*
1843. 43pp. Three editions are known, although the 'third' may
rather be a new issue of the second edition, which came out in 1848.
Lithographs by Rowe make a pleasant frontispiece for the first two
editions (which are similar but not identical) and a lithograph by
Day & Son decorates the third.

42. **The Whole Game of Cricket** *by an old Batsman. London.* [c. 1844.]
J. Neal, 61 St. John's Square. 31pp. A couple of pages form a
concession to tennis and fives. At about the same time as this treatise
appeared, another edition was published by Bowman in Newcastle.

43. **The Register of Cricket for Hingham,** *by an old player — Thomas*
Driver. Printed by Matchett, Stevenson & Matchett. Norwich, 1844.
36pp. The Register contains scores of matches dating back to 1802.
Norfolk tends to get overlooked a little in the writings on early
cricket; much of interest took place. **Rules of Lynn Cricket Club**
(1833), a 12-page pamphlet, is another out-of-the-way scarce item.

44. **Audley End Cricket book:** *being the scores of matches played on the lawn in front of the house from the 1st of May 1842 to the 31st August 1844. Privately printed G. Youngman, Saffron Walden, 1844.* 40pp. The copy at Lord's is inscribed: 'R. Ringwood. A present from the Honourable Richard Cornwallis Neville, eldest son of Lord Braybrooke, Audley End.'

Ringwood was the professional employed at Audley End for many years. A good bowler, in later life he partnered Tom Hayward the elder in running a cricket shop in Cambridge.

45. **Lillywhite's Illustrated hand-book of cricket;** *containing portraits of Pilch; Box; A. Mynn, Esq; C. Taylor, Esq; Lillywhite; Cobbett; G. H. Langdon, Esq; R. Kynaston, Esq; also the laws of cricket . . . edited by 'A Cantab'. Frederick William Lillywhite. Ackermann, London, 1844 & Mason, Brighton.* 22pp. There was a second edition in the same year. Both editions had issues with four portraits (the professionals only) and issues with one portrait (Lillywhite). A facsimile reprint appeared in **Chronicles of Cricket** (1888).

46. **The cricketer's companion,** *containing the scores of the ground and principal matches of cricket, played at Lord's and other grounds in the season 1843. William Denison. Published by W. Clement at the Office of 'Bell's Life', Strand, London, in the week ending April 7th, 1844.* 2 + iv + 54pp. There were six issues, covering four seasons, with different publishers: Clement was followed by Sherwood, Simpkin and Marshall. One of the printers was William Stevens, at Bell Yard, Temple Bar. Two editions appeared for the season 1843, two for 1844, and one each for 1845 and 1846. Date information appears to differ between the cloth cover, paper wrapper and title page of most editions. A way out of the confusion is to consult an article by Rowland Bowen in 'The Cricket Quarterly', vol.I, no.4, of 1963.

In his introduction to the penultimate edition, Denison relates a fascinating tale of misfortune:

> Another year has passed, and once more the author greets his 'Brethren of the Bat,' accompanied with an apology for the delay which has occurred in the renewal of that annual greeting. An unlooked-for circumstance rendered the postponement of the re-appearance of the 'Cricketer's Companion' a matter of necessity, for even upon that publication has the late railway mania had an operation. A considerable portion of the copy for the present number of the series the author had prepared and left at the house of a friend in town, and not having any immediate cause to visit the house in the early part of the spring, he did not call for

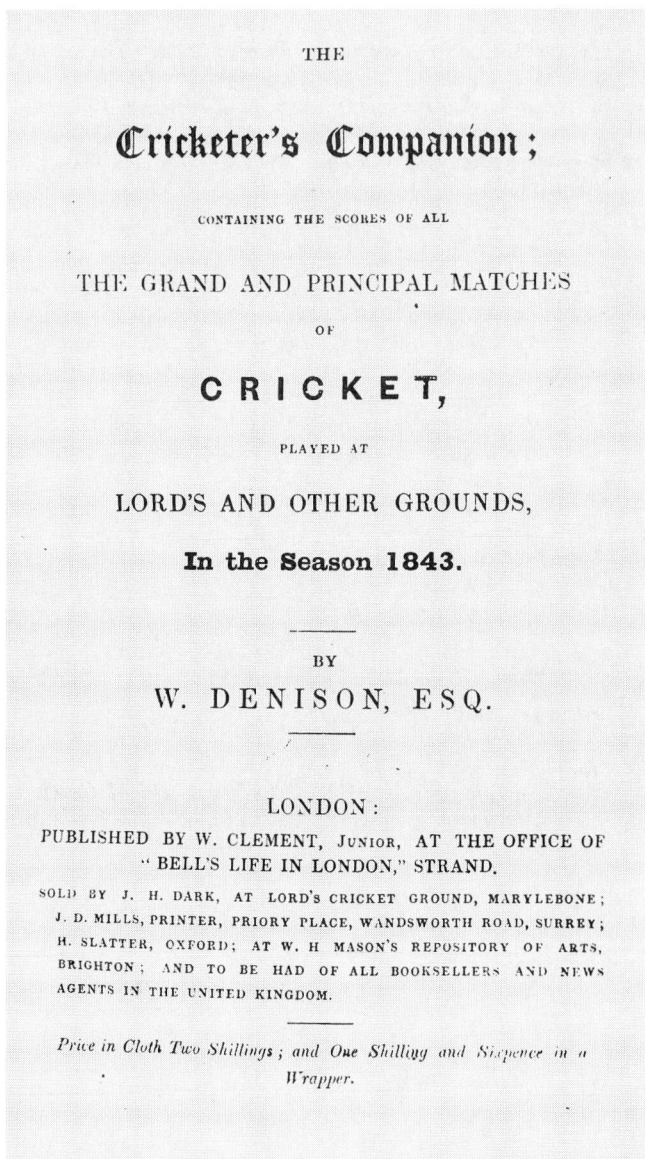

THE

Cricketer's Companion;

CONTAINING THE SCORES OF ALL

THE GRAND AND PRINCIPAL MATCHES

OF

CRICKET,

PLAYED AT

LORD'S AND OTHER GROUNDS,

In the Season 1843.

BY

W. DENISON, ESQ.

LONDON:

PUBLISHED BY W. CLEMENT, Junior, AT THE OFFICE OF
" BELL'S LIFE IN LONDON," STRAND.

SOLD BY J. H. DARK, AT LORD'S CRICKET GROUND, MARYLEBONE;
J. D. MILLS, PRINTER, PRIORY PLACE, WANDSWORTH ROAD, SURREY;
H. SLATTER, OXFORD; AT W. H MASON'S REPOSITORY OF ARTS,
BRIGHTON; AND TO BE HAD OF ALL BOOKSELLERS AND NEWS
AGENTS IN THE UNITED KINGDOM.

Price in Cloth Two Shillings ; and One Shilling and Sixpence in a
Wrapper.

See item 46

some two months. When he did, he found to his regret that his friend, having embroiled himself as the member of 'Provisional Committees,' had suddenly gone abroad, having previously intimated that so soon as each of his brother committeemen should think proper to put down their shares of a sufficient subscription to pay the liabilities he would return and hand over his proportion in common with the rest. Hoping that this proceeding would have come to pass within a reasonable period, the author awaited the return of his friend, so that he might obtain the MS., which had been placed, for especial safety, under lock and key. The moment for the realization of that hope has not yet arrived. Hence the delay, and the reader will peruse a work which has for a *second* time been prepared for the press, with a variety of matters omitted which would have been included but for the temporary loss alluded to. The majority of the matches nevertheless have been secured, though much statistical information is necessarily wanting.

The Author trusts, notwithstanding these omissions, that sufficient will be found in the 'Companion for 1846' to preserve the interest which his friends and companions in the game have been pleased to state that its yearly appearance has hitherto created.

Portland Terrace, Wandsworth Road,

July 14, 1846.

47. **Cricket: Sketches of the Players** *by W. Denison, Esq. Author of "The Cricketer's Companion". London, 1846. Simpkin, Marshall & Co., Stationers' Hall Court, Ludgate Hill.* 76pp. Thirteen other suppliers are named on the title page. The first real cricket reporter reviews the players of his day and one of an earlier period, Alfred Mynn.

The book has been reprinted in **Chronicles of Cricket** (1888) and in **The Middle Ages of Cricket** (1949), edited and introduced by John Arlott.

48. **The Cricketer's Handbook** *in Three Parts. I. History and Chronology of Cricket. II. Instructions for the Game. III. The Revised Laws. By the author of "Training for Pedestrianism and Wrestling", "British Boxing", etc. London.* [c.1845.] *W. M. Clark, 17, Warwick Lane (Clark's Sporting Hand-Books) and sold by all Booksellers. Printed at Steam-Press of W. M. Clark, Red Lion Court, Fleet St., London.* 56pp. Clark's Handbook is a desirable item. If there were 15 editions published (which is unlikely, to say the least), only five appear to have survived: two unnumbered, of which one is presumably the first, 10th, 14th (a copy is listed in the British Museum Catalogue but is missing from the shelves) and 15th. There may, of

EXPLANATORY DIAGRAM OF THE GAME OF CRICKET.

The Batsmen, or Striker.   2. The Bowler.   **3.** The Wicket-keeper.   4. Point (of bat).   5. Short Slip.   6. Long Stop.   7. Long Slip.   8. Middle Wicket.   9. Long Field straight off.   10. Long Field straight on.   11. Long Field cover to point and Middle Wicket.   12. Long Field to the Hip.   13. 13. Umpires.   14. Scorers.   **X X** Bowling Crease.   † † Popping Crease.
The outline Scene is sketched from Lord's Ground, Marylebone, and exhibits the Pavilion, the New Tennis Court, &c.   * The Entrance Gate.

An illustration from Clark's *Cricketer's Handbook*: see item 48.

course, be other unnumbered, or indeed numbered, editions in existence to complement them.

By the 10th edition, the title page had altered slightly: the phrase 'by the author of' had been replaced by 'Tenth Edition (Corrected to June, 1849) By a Member of the Marylebone Cricket Club'. The year is handwritten, which suggests that Clark was planning to issue the same handbook, with little or no amendment, annually. Alternatively, there could have been doubt as to the publication date, and concern that the details of some of the inclusions might be superseded. The edition is thought to have come out in 1850 and by this time Clark refers to himself as 'William Mark Clark, Wholesale Bookseller, Warwick Lane, Paternoster Row'. His printing works, at 10 Red Lion Court, had been taken over by G. Lawrence, who later moved to 29 Farringdon Street. Clark apparently needed extra room to house his expanding business, which involved marketing his many

CLARK'S
CRICKETER'S
HANDBOOK.

IN THREE PARTS,

I.—HISTORY AND CHRONOLOGY OF CRICKET.

II.—INSTRUCTIONS FOR THE GAME.

III.—THE REVISED LAWS.

FIFTEENTH EDITION.

CORRECTED TO THE PRESENT TIME

BY A MEMBER OF THE MARYLEBONE

CRICKET CLUB.

LONDON:

WILLIAM MARK CLARK,

WHOLESALE BOOKSELLER,

16 & 17, WARWICK LANE, PATERNOSTER ROW;

AND SOLD BY ALL BOOKSELLERS.

PRICE SIXPENCE

See item 48

handbooks, Orphean Warblers with 2,500 popular songs, Ciceronian Reciters and a lengthy list of melodrama, criminology and tales of derring-do. He therefore acquired the premises at 16 Warwick Lane to ease the strain on No. 17.

The 14th edition of the Handbook came out in 1858 and the 15th around 1859, so there is a logic to the numbering of those issues if we note the year of the first production and assume that Clark was then trying to give the impression of a continuing annual publication. He hoped, perhaps, that memories were short regarding the year that the 10th edition first appeared, though, as we have seen, the year of completion, 1849, was handwritten on the title page; consequently, if unsold copies were later updated by the insertion of a different year, there might have been little to dispel the idea of regular sequential numbering. Much of this is, of course, supposition and interpretation yet it is based on practices that were not uncommon with the trade at the time.

On the final page of the first edition of the Handbook, Clark advertises his handbooks on Pedestrianism and Wrestling, Boxing, a book of 100 Sporting Songs and, most intriguingly, one of the 'lost' items of cricketana:

To Hang in Parlours, Club-Rooms, etc.

Neatly mounted on Canvass [*sic*] and varnished, on a Roller,

Price One Shilling and Sixpence,

Clark's Cricketer's Companion

This beautiful and closely printed sheet contains a Historical Summary and Chronology of Cricket; detailed instructions for every fieldsman in the game, and the Revised Laws, forming an unique epitome of 'things worth knowing' by every Cricketer.

John Goulstone, to whom every cricket historian owes a debt, unearthed the fact that Clark died in 1861 and that his business was continued by his wife, Elizabeth.

49. **The Laws of Cricket, as revised and amended by the Mary-le-bonne** [sic] **Club,** *June 2, 1845, with Notes, explanatory of the Usages of the Game, and Practical Hints To The Young Cricketer. By a member of the Toronto Club. Toronto — MDCCCXLV. Printed and Published at the Herald Office, 36½, Yonge St.* 30pp. To write of this work as exceptionally rare would be an understatement. A

THE LAWS OF CRICKET,

AS REVISED AND AMENDED BY THE MARY-LE-BONNE CLUB,

June 2, 1845 ;

WITH

NOTES,

𝔈𝔵𝔭𝔩𝔞𝔫𝔞𝔱𝔬𝔯𝔶 𝔬𝔣 𝔱𝔥𝔢 𝔘𝔰𝔞𝔤𝔢𝔰 𝔬𝔣 𝔱𝔥𝔢 𝔊𝔞𝔪𝔢,

AND

PRACTICAL HINTS

TO

THE YOUNG CRICKETER.

BY A MEMBER OF THE TORONTO CLUB.

TORONTO—MDCCCXLV.

See item 49

copy was sold at the auction of J. W. Goldman's collection in 1966 for £25. No other has been seen since in the market-place.

The work was compiled by G. A. Barber and has a dedication to William Boulton, Mayor of Toronto. The book which was once in Goldman's possession was a presentation copy to His Excellency, the Governor-General of Canada, Charles T. Metcalfe. Metcalfe's tenure (1843–45) was relatively short because of ill health; it is conceivable that the book was a farewell gift.

50. **Felix on the bat:** *being a scientific inquiry into the use of the cricket bat; together with the history and use of the catapulta ... also the laws of cricket, as revised by the Marylebone Club.* [Nicholas Wanostrocht (Felix).] *Baily Bros., Cornhill, 1845.* 40pp. 'Felix on the bat' has the distinction of being the first book of cricket instruction to be illustrated with coloured lithographs. There were two more editions at five-year intervals. Gerald Brodribb's **The Art of Nicholas Felix** (1985) is the definitive survey of his work as an artist and author. Brodribb lists several appetizing titles: A. M. Broadley's **Some Memorials of Nicholas Felix** (1912); **A succinct account of the Eleven of England, selected to contend in the great cricket matches of the north, for the year 1847**; **The Doings of the eleven ...** (2 vols, dated 1851 and 1852); and, apparently, an unpublished **Treatise on the Cut.** Apart from, possibly, 'A succinct account ...' the items are unique and, as such, virtually impossible to procure.

Any of the three editions of 'Felix on the bat' fetches a high price in the auction-room or the bookshop, not least because of the distinctive lithographs by G. F. Watts. Felix also wrote **The Cricket Bat and how to use it** in 1861, some copies of which had a variant date on the title page, 1860; this book of instruction had a second issue and a second edition.

51. **The Manual of Cricket;** *with numerous illustrations, comprising The Laws of the Game, some account of its history, and of the progressive improvements made therein, directions and instructions in the practice and play of this manly and athletic exercise, and suggestions as to the variations and applications of the play, so as to afford satisfactory recreation to small numbers of players. The whole being intended as A Complete Cricketer's Guide: to which is added the body, and all that is important of 'Felix on the Bat'. By Alexander D. Paterson. New York, 1847. Published by Berford & Co., No. 2*

THE

MANUAL OF CRICKET;

WITH

NUMEROUS ILLUSTRATIONS,

COMPRISING

THE LAWS OF THE GAME, SOME
ACCOUNT OF ITS HISTORY, AND OF THE
PROGRESSIVE IMPROVEMENTS MADE THEREIN,
DIRECTIONS AND INSTRUCTIONS IN THE PRACTICE AND
PLAY OF THIS MANLY AND ATHLETIC EXERCISE, AND SUGGES-
TIONS AS TO THE VARIATIONS AND APPLICATIONS OF THE
PLAY, SO AS TO AFFORD SATISFACTORY RECREA-
TION TO SMALL NUMBERS OF PLAYERS.

THE WHOLE BEING INTENDED AS

A Complete Cricketer's Guide:

TO WHICH IS ADDED THE BODY, AND
ALL THAT IS IMPORTANT OF

"FELIX ON. THE BAT."

BY ALEXANDER D. PATERSON.

NEW YORK:

PUBLISHED BY BERFORD & CO.,
No. 2 Astor House,
1847.

See item 51

THE

CRICKETERS' MANUAL,

FOR 1848,

CONTAINING A BRIEF REVIEW OF THE

CHARACTER, RISE, AND PROGRESS

OF THE MANLY AND NOBLE

GAME OF CRICKET

AND

THE LAWS

APPERTAINING TO IT,

AS RECENTLY REVISED BY THE MARYLEBONE CLUB;

ALSO, A CAREFULLY CONSTRUCTED

ANALYTICAL TABLE,

OF THE DOINGS OF

140 PROFESSIONAL & AMATEUR PLAYERS

DURING THE LAST SEASON; THE

SITUATION AND STRENGTH OF THE METROPOLITAN AND SUBURBAN CLUBS;

EXTENT OF GROUNDS;

MR. BARON ALDERSON'S RECOMMENDATION OF CRICKET;

Together with a variety of useful and requisite information to all those who patronize this truly national pastime,

BY "BAT,"

AUTHOR OF REMINISCENCIES OF CELEBRATED PLAYERS, ETC.

ENTERED AT STATIONERS' HALL.

Price 6d. ; bound in Cloth, 1s.

London:

PUBLISHED BY WILLIAM BRITTAIN, 45, PATERNOSTER ROW,

And may be obtained of R. DARK, Lord's Ground ; HOUGHTON, Kennington Oval; ACKERMANN'S, Strand; H. SLATTER, Oxford; FENNER, Cambridge ; MASON's Repository of Arts, Brighton ; and of all Booksellers and Dealers in Cricketing paraphernalia throughout the United Kingdom.

1848.

See item 52

Astor House. Truss & Graham, Printers, No. 22, Spruce St. N.Y.
163pp. This must qualify, surely, as one of the longest titles on a
cricket book, comprising more than one hundred words, inclusive of
the publishing details. Mr. Paterson borrowed material from Felix,
with or without permission, and dedicated his long-winded treatise
to 'Henry Jessop, Esq. President, the Officers and the Members of
the St. George Cricket Club of New York'.

52. **The cricketers' manual, for 1848,** *containing a brief review of the
character, rise, and progress of the manly and noble game of cricket
and the laws . . . by "Bat"* [Charles Box]. *William Brittain, 1848.
45, Paternoster Row.* 39pp. This handy little manual contains useful
and often unexpected information: lists and sketches of players,
curiosities, elements of the character of the game, principal Metro-
politan clubs and grounds. In 1848 there were two issues, in 1849
one, in 1850 two again and in 1851 four. In the 1851 manual, Box
refers to 'four editions' issued previously; either he was thinking of
the two issues for 1850 (which had a number of differences) as two
separate editions, or he had miscounted, or there was an earlier book,
say for 1847, which has not been seen. In his 'preface to the fifth
edition', Box comments also on the size of the original manual 'three
years ago'; which argues, if not conclusively, against the latter
supposition.

   Baily Brothers, who published 'Felix on the Bat', did the same for
the manuals from 1849, with the exception of the final two issues
for 1851, which were produced by Joseph Myers. Rowland Bowen,
in his article on 'The Cricketer's Manual by "Bat" ' ('The Cricket
Quarterly', vol.7, no. 4), wonders if there could have been piracy.

   G. Neville Weston produced a short bibliography of 'The Cricketer's Manual' in 1936 which, as a collector's item, is much
sought-after, but as a bibliographical tool should be treated with
caution, as Weston assumes that different-colour paper covers denote
separate issues.

53. **Rules of the Haigh Colliery Cricket Club.** *Haigh, the Club, 1849.*
Padwick refers to an entry in **Bibliotheca Lindesiana,** vol. I.

54. **Descriptive key to Mason's national print of a cricket match
between Sussex and Kent, 1849.** *Brighton. W. H. Mason, London.
Gambert, 1849.* 23pp. The key identifies well-known figures who
were actually at the match and also those that were supposed to have
been. The print is often seen, the pamphlet only rarely. A copy sold

for £110 at a recent Phillips sale, which could be construed as a bargain.

55. **The Young Cricketer's Guide,** *containing full directions for playing the noble and manly game of cricket by William Lillywhite. To which is added the Laws of the game, with the latest alterations, and some brief remarks upon fifty of the most celebrated gentlemen and players in England. The whole collected and edited by Frederick Lillywhite, Junr. F. Lillywhite.* [1849-1866.] 32pp. The Lillywhite Guides, of which perhaps only three or four complete sets exist, are a bibliographical quagmire. It may be simplest to think of the run as comprising 22 editions plus two extra issues, though for a detailed numbering sequence one can consult Padwick's **Bibliography.** A 23rd edition, which is labelled as such, is in fact the third issue of John Lillywhite's **Cricketer's Companion** (1867), with which the Guide was incorporated. Rockley Wilson owned two copies of the 23rd edition, but they varied in the colour of the covers and in the number of pages carrying advertisements.

56. **Cricketer's Companion.** *Lillywhite. Scores. Published John Lilly-white* [initially]. [1865-1885.] There were 21 editions, covering two decades. Kent & Co. became joint publishers in 1867, when brother Fred's **Young Cricketer's Guide** joined hands. In 1880, the Companion became **John and James Lillywhite's Cricketer's Companion** (James being a cousin of John and Fred) and then, in 1883, solely **James Lillywhite's Cricketer's Companion.** From 1886, the Companion (the so-called 'Green Lillywhite' because of the colour of its cover) was absorbed into the **Cricketers' annual** (the 'Red Lillywhite'), published by James, *brother* of Fred and John.

57. **Cricketers' annual;** *edited by Charles W. Alcock.* [James] *Lillywhite, Frowde & Co.* [1872-1900.] The partners publishing the 'Red Lillywhite' changed several times. There were three editions for 1872, and two each for 1884 and 1885. Some copies for 1873 have errata slips and some do not; there may be other years that have similar differences. Consequently, it would appear that there were 34 separate issues.

An article on 'The Green and Red Lillywhites', by Rowland Bowen, is to be found in 'The Cricket Quarterly', vol. I, no. 1, of 1963. It contains valuable biographical as well as bibliographical information.

THE

𝔜oung 𝔠ricketer's 𝔤uide,

CONTAINING

FULL DIRECTIONS FOR PLAYING THE NOBLE
AND MANLY GAME OF

CRICKET,

BY WILLIAM LILLYWHITE.

TO WHICH IS ADDED

𝔗he 𝔏aws of the 𝔤ame, with the latest 𝔄lterations,

AND

SOME BRIEF REMARKS UPON FIFTY OF THE MOST
CELEBRATED GENTLEMEN AND PLAYERS
IN ENGLAND.

THE WHOLE COLLECTED AND EDITED BY
BY FREDERICK LILLYWHITE, Jun.

LONDON:
PUBLISHED BY F. LILLYWHITE, LORD'S CRICKET GROUND,
MARYLEBONE.

See item 55

58. **The Illustrated Laws of Cricket, as revised by The Marylebone Club, 1849,** *with copious explanatory remarks . . . to which is added an essay On cricket by Ned Rub* [pseudonym of Burden] *with the alteration of the laws and an abstract of the averages of 1848. James W. Burden. publ. W. Gibbs, 1849.* 30pp. Burden, the cricket reporter for 'Bell's Life in London', dedicated this booklet to 'Felix, by kind permission, June 1, 1849'. Burden compiled **The Cricketer's Chronicle** three years later.

59. **The Cricketers' Manual** *containing the Rules of the Marylebone Club. No. 25 of Dipple's Handbooks. Edwin Dipple, 42, Holywell St., Strand, London.* [c.1850.] 16pp. The Manual contains a list of the authorized umpires, including J. W. Burden at 15 Gt. College Street, Camden Town and F. Pilch, bat and ball maker of Canterbury.

    The introduction refers to 'the royal and noble patronage this sport has enjoyed. We may instance the late William the Fourth to whom the Royal Clarence Cricket Club at Hampton owes its birth and name.'

    A Thomas Dibdin ditty provides added flavour.

60. **Brecon Town and Garrison Cricket Club.** *Rules and Regulations the same as those of the Marylebone Club. 1850.* Included is a list of more than 50 subscribers, among them Col. Lloyd V. Watkins, MP, Capt. Lord A. Russell of the Rifle Brigade, T. Williams (late Mayor), J. Davies, jeweller, and H. Shum, chemist. 'Bob' Harragan, the Welsh cricket historian, brought this item to light; it resides in the Brecon Museum, together with the Club's scorebook, commencing in 1846, and the South Wales Club scorebook, covering the period 1859 to 1865. He also supplied much of the following information.

    John Lloyd senior, founder of the Brecon Club, produced **The English Country Gentleman, His Sports and Pastimes,** which was published in London by Langman & Co. and in Llandovery by W. Rees. There was a first edition in 1849 and a second in 1852; cricket finds its way into a poem therein.

    There is also a printed membership list of Raglan C.C., dating from about 1835–45.

    Newport Cricket Club (President, Samuel Homfray, Esq.) published a list of 70 members in 1856 and in the mid-1880s Evan Williams of Market Place, Bangor, printed the **Rules of the Bangor**

Cricket Club *(High Street, Bangor, Established 1867)*. This comprised eight pages.

Glamorgan C.C.C.'s first manuscript minute book dates from 1889, and by 1892 a yearbook was being published by T. Page Wood and Co., Cricket and Tennis outfitters of Cardiff. **The Invincible Cricket Guide** was produced in Swansea in 1895.

Welsh cricket books thus had a chequered start. However, it is worth mentioning that there is much interesting information to be found in **The Cricketer's Manual for the Border Counties,** *containing a review and averages for the season 1869, published by Askew Roberts, Woodall and Venables of Oswestry.*

61. **The Cricket Field; or the history and the science of cricket.** *By the author of "The principles of scientific batting" — James Pycroft. Longman, Brown, Green and Longmans, London, 1851.* 242pp. There were nine editions and a second issue of the fifth edition. The ninth edition was issued by the Cricket Press in 1887. An American edition was also produced, by Mayhew and Baker in Boston in 1859. Finally, there was a 1922 edition, with some notes by H. H. Stephenson, captain of the English team which played in Australia in 1861–62, and an introduction together with copious annotations from F. S. Ashley-Cooper. This edition was also produced as a limited issue of 100 for subscribers.

62. **Lansdown Cricket Club Matches** [1825 to 1851]. *Printed and published for the Club by R. E. Peach, 1852.* The Club started originally with James Pycroft and his school fellows playing on Charmbury Down. It later moved to Lansdown, where the adults joined in.

63. **Matches played by the Haileybury Cricket Club, 1840–51.** *Hertford, 1852. Printed by G. and S. E. Simson.* 82pp. This item is hard to acquire.

64. **Cricket Notes,** *with a letter containing practical hints, by W. Clark, William Bolland, Trelawny Saunders, 1851.* iv + 155pp. The notes comprise reminiscences, commentary and essays. Clark was, in fact, William Clark*e*, who launched the All-England Eleven. Bolland was elected 'Permanent President' of I Zingari.

65. **How to Play Clarke:** *Being an attempt to unravel the Mysteries of the Ball, and to show what defence and hitting are to be employed against this celebrated bowler. By the author of 'Felix on the Bat'.*

[N. Wanostrocht—'Felix']. *London, 1852. Baily Brothers, Royal Exchange Buildings, Cornhill.* 16pp. The title is self-explanatory, featuring the ploys of the great Nottinghamshire and All-England bowler, William Clarke. The booklet was reprinted in 1922, with an introduction from F. S. Ashley-Cooper. Only two or three copies are believed to exist, of which one sold for £320 at a recent auction.

66. **Cricketer's handbook: a complete guide to field sports in general.** *Containing all the Laws and Rules, with full directions for playing Cricket, by single and double wicket, the Game of Trap, Bat and Ball, the Essex Trap Ball, etc. 'A Member of the M.C.C.' W. G. Kerton, 1852.* 16pp. A familiar pattern is reconstructed.

67. **Nottingham cricket matches, from 1771 to 1853:** *with an introductory chapter, descriptive of the local history of the game; and brief sketches of the principal players. John Frost Sutton. Nottingham, The Author, 1853.* 118pp. A second edition was produced by the Sutton Brothers in 1859, with an additional 22 pages covering matches from 1771 to 1859. A. R. Sutton gave his name to a third edition, treating the period 1771 to 1865, issued in the latter year.

There are a number of cricket references to be found in J. F. Sutton's **The Date book of remarkable and memorable events connected with Nottingham and its neighbourhood, 1750–1850,** published by R. Sutton in Nottingham and Simpkin and Marshall in London in 1852. There were also two further editions of this work, in 1880 and 1884.

68. **Matches of the Calcutta Cricket Club 1844–1854.** *Free School Press, Calcutta, 1854.* 4 + 120pp. If this is not the earliest book of printed cricket scores to appear outside England, it is certainly one of the first. As a periodical, however, 'The Bengal Sporting Magazine' of 1834–42, whose compilation was conducted by J. H. Stocqueler and at another time by William Rushton, included much cricket. Echoes of the Raj are sounded by such matches as 'Barrackpore with three from Dum Dum v The Calcutta Club', played on 28th December 1844, and 'Calcutta v Hooghly and Chinsurah C.C.', played on 14th December 1852.

69. The first Australian Cricket Annual was **The Australian Cricketer's Guide for 1856-7,** edited by H. Biers and W. Fairfax and published in Melbourne by W. Fairfax & Co. in 1857. A succession of annuals followed — all short-lived — which were edited and published by

AUSTRALIAN

CRICKETER'S GUIDE

FOR 1856-7.

EDITED BY H. BIERS & W. FAIRFAX.

MELBOURNE:

W. FAIRFAX & CO., PRINTERS AND PUBLISHERS.

STEAM PRESS, 78, COLLINS STREET, EAST.

GEELONG: FRANKS & JACKSON.   SYDNEY: J. L. SHERRIFF.

HOBART TOWN: WALCH & SONS.   LAUNCESTON: A. PUTHIE.

ADELAIDE: E. S. WIGG.   AND ALL BOOKSELLERS.

PRICE TWO SHILLINGS & SIXPENCE.

See item 69

HAANDBOG

I

CRICKET og LANGBOLD.

UDGIVET

AF

"DEN KJØBENHAVNSKE BOLDSPILKLUB".

KJØBENHAVN.

C. C. LOSE'S FORLAG.

THIELES BOGTRYKKERI.

1866.

See item 69

entrepreneurial souls whose aspirations failed to be matched by those who were meant to buy their product. A full listing by Ken Piesse (part of a thesis at the Royal Melbourne Institute of Technology) is printed in 'The Journal of the Cricket Society', vol. 11, nos. 1 and 2. Previous issues (vol. 9, no. 4; vol. 10, nos. 1 and 2) tell the story in more detail. Padwick notes a separate 66-page typescript of the thesis: there are five copies only. Piesse writes of 'perhaps the rarest of all the early Australian annuals, **The Queensland Cricketers' Guide and Annual for 1884–5,**' that 'no copy of this annual which was printed by Trimble and Co. of Brisbane at 1/6d has been found.'

Rowland Bowen in his book **Cricket: a History of its growth and development throughout the World** (1970), quotes the **Auckland Cricketers' Trip to the South in 1873-4** as the first known cricket publication in New Zealand; while **Pavilion Echoes from the South, 1884–5,** *by the Twelve,* concentrates on the same kind of operation. In 'The Cricket Quarterly', vol. 7, no. 4, the same author catalogues the South African cricket annuals, starting with **The South African Cricketing Guide 1871-2,** a 24-page publication from Capetown, and continuing with the **Natal Cricketer's Annual,** which changed its name to **The South African Cricketer's Annual** in the 1888/89 season. It is also worth noting **The Tournament Chronicle,** whose publication resulted from a series of matches played in Port Elizabeth: nine issues were brought out in 1884–85, and these subsequently appeared in one volume.

From more unlikely sources, early cricket offerings have arrived in the form of a technical treatise in German from the Carlsruhe Cricket Club, dated 1874, a manual of 1866 in Danish, with the title **Haandbog i cricket og langbold,** and, much more surprisingly, an instructional book in Spanish called **La tranca: juego atletico,** by J. W. Williams, that was published in Buenos Aires in 1881.

70. **Colney Hatch Cricket Club.** *Rules and regulations of the Colney Hatch Cricket Club held at the Orange Tree Inn, Colney Hatch, established the 30th day of August, 1853. Barnet, W. Baldock. 1856.* 7pp. This is the sort of item that one might come across while rummaging at a colporteur's stand.

71. **Cricket made easy:** *the standard authority, giving plain and perfect directions both of the theory and practice of this noble outdoor sport; so that it can be perfectly learned without a master. New York, 1857.*

Advance Publishing Co. 64pp. Another edition was issued in the 1870s. A copy of this treatise is in the New York Public Library.

72. **A manual of cricket and baseball;** *containing plans for laying out the grounds, plans for forming clubs, etc., to which are added rules and regulations for Cricket adopted by the Marylebone Cricket Club; also rules and regulations which govern several celebrated baseball clubs. Mayhew and Baker, 208, Washington St., Boston, 1858. A Mudge & Sons, Printers, 34, School St.* 24pp. For a second edition one year later, cricket and baseball were divided into two books, namely **The cricket player's pocket companion** and **The base-ball player's pocket companion:** 'This has been rendered necessary on account of many additions which have been made to both making it impossible to bring them into one book of a size and price to meet the wants of all lovers of these now very fashionable sports.'

73. **The Canadian cricketers' guide and review of the past season.** There were three issues only: the one for 1858, which was produced by members of the St. Catherines Cricket Club (at St. Catherines, Constitution Office) and consists of 74 pages, is the hardest of the three to obtain. Both the 1876 and 1877 issues were compiled and produced by T. D. Phillipps and H. J. Campbell of Ottawa.

74. **The International Cricket Match played Oct. 1859 in the Elysian Fields at Hoboken on the ground of the St. George's Cricket Club.** *John B. Irving. New York, 1859. Vinten, Printer, 100, Nassau Street.* x + 31pp. The eleven pros from England played 22 from clubs in the U.S.A. Mr. Charles Vinten (the printer?) umpired with John Lillywhite. The substance of Dr. Irving's report was printed in 'The Charleston Courier', a daily journal.

75. **Beadle's dime book of cricket;** *a desirable cricketer's companion, containing complete instructions in the elements of bowling, batting and fielding, also the revised laws of the game, remarks on the duties of umpires, etc. etc. Editor: Henry Chadwick. I. P. Beadle & Co., New York, 1860.* 40pp. A copy is interred in the New York Public Library. Football was included for another edition in 1866 and the number of pages increased by ten.

Chadwick's **American cricket manual** (1873) was published by Robert M. de Witt, whose name headed the title-page for another edition in 1879. The same firm also brought out a handbook on

THE CRICKET FIELD.

THE

CRICKET PLAYER'S

POCKET COMPANION.

CONTAINING

PLANS FOR LAYING OUT THE GROUNDS,

FORMING CLUBS, &c., &c.,

TO WHICH ARE ADDED

RULES AND REGULATIONS FOR CRICKET,

ADOPTED BY THE

MARY-LE-BONE CLUB.

BOSTON:

MAYHEW & BAKER, 208 WASHINGTON STREET.

1859.

See item 72

LOCKYER AT THE WICKET.

An illustration from *The English Cricketers' Trip to Canada and the United States*: see item 78.

See item 78

cricket and lacrosse in about 1880, as part of their Standard series, and this in turn saw another edition at about the same time with the name of Wehman on the title-page.

76. **Gauntlet's cricketers' record,** *containing the full scores of all the great matches played during the season; with the averages of the players, together with a list of batsmen who have obtained 100 runs and over.* [Gauntlet, Sevenoaks.] Padwick gives two seasons for the annual: 1859 and 1860. In the bibliography of **The Dawn of Cricket,** by H. T. Waghorn, there is an entry for 1869, which would appear to be an error.

77. **How to play cricket** *(Family Herald Handy Books). Stevens.* [c.1859.] 39pp. Two later editions incorporate football. The format of this book follows the pattern of guides such as J. Blackwood's **Take my advice on games and how to play them** (c.1853, plus later editions).

78. **The English Cricketers' Trip to Canada and The United States** *by Fred. Lillywhite. London, 1860. F. Lillywhite, 15, Kennington Oval, S; Kent & Co., 23, Paternoster Row, E.C.* viii + 68pp. A colourful account of the first tour unfolds, with many illustrations, and statistics from the tent of the travelling reporter himself. The wintry weather for the last match near New York caused the players to wear great-coats and mittens.

79. **Cricket Scores and Biographies of Celebrated Cricketers, from 1746.** [15 vols.] *1862.* Frederick Lillywhite published the first four volumes and, typically, put his name above the title, complemented by an audacious note, 'To the Cricketing World', at the front of vol.I, in which he takes the major credit for the compilation. The great bulk of all the work was carried out by Arthur Haygarth, to whom cricket's historians should doff their caps with gratitude. These first four volumes of the series are the hardest to find as the impressions were destroyed in an act of anger at the slowness of the sale.

The M.C.C. took over the financial burden and helped secure the continuation of the run. The final volume, no.15, is composed entirely of biographical notices of cricketers and was brought up to date by F. S. Ashley-Cooper, based on notes of the late Arthur Haygarth to the end of 1898.

FREDERICK LILLYWHITE'S

CRICKET SCORES

AND

BIOGRAPHIES

OF

CELEBRATED CRICKETERS,

FROM

1746 to 1826.

VOL. I.

LONDON:

PUBLISHED BY FREDERICK LILLYWHITE,
THE OVAL, KENNINGTON, SURREY.

1862.

See item 79

The universally accepted value of 'S & B' is shown by the number of indexes in existence. A. L. Ford compiled an index to vols. 1–13 (biographies only), which was published by the Cricket Office in 1895. He also provided a 27-page typescript index to vol.14, which forms part of his collection held at Lord's. J. B. Payne felt compelled much later to give a similar treatment to all the first-class matches in the series, together with 229 biographies indexed from vol. 14. There is also an index of minor matches up to 1878, assiduously compiled by G. B. Buckley, the 136-page typescript again being kept in the M.C.C. Library at Lord's. Finally, there exists a huge handwritten leather-bound index, containing scorecards and much else peripheral to the main body of the work, put together by A. J. Gaston. According to the preface, three copies exist, which is a staggering thought when one considers the enormous mental effort required to scribe the whole thing twice more. One is reminded of the massive 18-inch-thick book kept by Gaston, containing, among other things, his personal collection of letters, signatures and score cards, that is mentioned by Irving Rosenwater in his splendid monograph **Alfred James Gaston, a study in Enthusiasm,** which was privately printed in a limited edition in 1975; and also of the 4 volumes of manuscript and cuttings that Haygarth compiled, not only relating to his own cricketing career but also to much else (these volumes are now at Lord's).

In 1857, W. H. Crockford's of Blackheath Rd., Greenwich, printed **A List of Matches to be published in F. Lillywhite's Large Work of Cricket Scores from 1746 to 1856 inclusive.**

80. **Cricket: with full instructions how to learn and how to play.** *(Young England's Cricket). Frederick Lillywhite. W. Twedie, 1862.* 32pp. As with this handbook, the ubiquitous Fred Lillywhite was involved with a **Pocket book of the Laws of Cricket,** which we are asked to believe eventually managed 60 editions, and also published accounts of **The Public School matches** that were compiled by Arthur Haygarth (John Lillywhite took the honours on the title-page of the last edition that was to be issued).

In 1857, in partnership with John Wisden, Fred Lillywhite co-published **An account of all the cricket matches played between Eton and Winchester; Westminster and Charterhouse; Rugby and Marlborough; and Marlborough and Cheltenham.** In 1865, in liaison with Ward, he brought out a **Cricketer's own register: score sheets and instructions.**

81. **The Handbook of Cricket** *by Edmund Routledge. (Routledge's Sixpenny Handbooks.) London, 1862. George Routledge and Sons, Broadway, Ludgate Hill, New York, 9, Lafayette Place and 416 Broome St.* 64pp. Seven editions are known up to 1869, and it is possible that others exist. The Handbook was translated into Dutch by L. Dekker in 1881: *Handleiding tot het cricketspel naar het Engelsch* (Haarlem, Bohn, 75pp.).

82. **The Cricket Tutor,** *by the author of 'The Cricket-field'. James Pycroft. Longman, Green, Longman, and Roberts, London, 1862.* viii + 85pp. The tutor is not only a practical treatise but also contains biographical snippets. A second edition came out in the same year.

83. **Cricket: the full scores of all the All-England, United, County and first-class eleven a side matches played in the season 1862.** *Richard Clarke Thorp. T. Lingard. Barnsley, 1862.* 88pp. Thorp is a useful reference for the year, providing pre-Wisden coverage. The price given on the title page is 1s/6d, while on the cover it is 1/–; which suggests there were some faint hearts at the marketing stage.

84. **The cabinet: a repository of facts, figures and fancies relating to the voyage of the "Great Britain" S.S. from Liverpool to Melbourne, with the Eleven of All England.** *Edited by Alexander Reid. J. Reid, Melbourne, 1862.* A photographic facsimile edition was produced in the 1970s in conjunction with the S.S. Great Britain Project. The 46 pages, featuring H. H. Stephenson's team, consisted of four issues of 'The Cabinet', printed originally in 1861.

85. **The trip to Australia: scraps from the diary of one of the twelve.** *Edward Mills Grace. W. H. Knight, 1864. Cox and Wyman.* 20pp. A. D. Taylor records that 'this pamphlet is in the form of a diary kept by E. M. Grace' of the 1863–64 tour led by George Parr. 'Curiously enough, it was printed unbeknown to the author, and it was not until some years later that he was aware of the fact.'

86. **A digest of cricketing facts and feats appertaining to the year 1862,** *to which are added two new songs from the notebook of 'Bat', also the laws of cricket as recently revised by the Marylebone Club. A Spectator, Esq.* [pseudonym]. *F. Platts. 1863.* iv + 62pp. 'Bat' (Charles Box) was fond of collecting cricketing songs, though whether

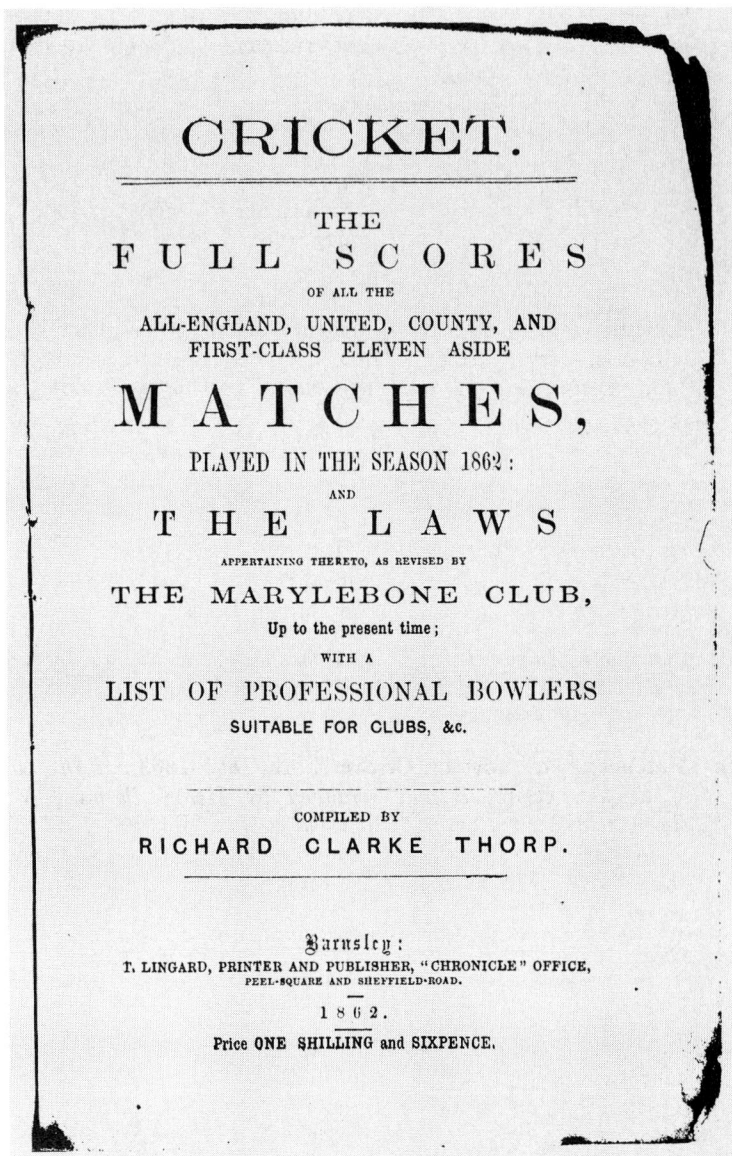

CRICKET.

THE
FULL SCORES
OF ALL THE
ALL-ENGLAND, UNITED, COUNTY, AND
FIRST-CLASS ELEVEN ASIDE
MATCHES,
PLAYED IN THE SEASON 1862:
AND
THE LAWS
APPERTAINING THERETO, AS REVISED BY
THE MARYLEBONE CLUB,
Up to the present time;
WITH A
LIST OF PROFESSIONAL BOWLERS
SUITABLE FOR CLUBS, &c.

COMPILED BY
RICHARD CLARKE THORP.

Barnsley:
T. LINGARD, PRINTER AND PUBLISHER, "CHRONICLE" OFFICE,
PEEL-SQUARE AND SHEFFIELD-ROAD.

1862.

Price ONE SHILLING and SIXPENCE.

See item 83

his acquisition matched his composition is difficult to say. The two generously donated here are: 'The cricketers' tent' and 'The cricket bat an emblem of peace'.

87. **The Cricket Chronicle for the season 1863:** *a record of matches played in 1863. Capt. W. Bayly. Publ. A. H. Baily & Co., London, 1863. Printed by Harrild, London.* v + 513pp. Some covers are dated 1864, but these are from the same issue. The Chronicle was intended to be an annual; inevitably, the high price (2s/6d) precluded a good sale.

   Perhaps Capt. Bayly was too ambitious in his scope, providing domestic coverage as well as matches in cricket's remoter climes (Brussels, Corfu, Dresden, Dieppe, Hamilton, Malta, Mauritius, Montreal, Rio de Janeiro, St. Petersburg, Toronto and Valparaiso).

88. **The cricketer's guide: a complete manual of the game of cricket.** *John Heywood, Manchester, 1863.* 36pp. There are eight listed editions, the last appearing in 1896. The edition of 1889 had a separate issue (1890?) with a different illustration. Later editions emanated from Deansgate and Ridgefield, Manchester; 2, Amen Corner, London, E.C.; 22, Paradise St., Liverpool; 33, Bridge St., Bristol; and also 1, Paternoster Buildings, London.

89. **Penny illustrated guide to the cricket field.** *Maddick and Pottage, 1863.* 16pp. This is a guide for those who understand better with pictures than with words.

90. **Matches of the Royston Cricket Club, 1855–1863** *and the Laws of Cricket. Compiled and arranged by Henry Perkins, M.A. Barrister-at-Law. Royston. Published by John Warren. 1864.* The preface intimates that the publication is the second edition. Apparently, the first edition contained 'Averages of the Players', which are now omitted. 'The Club, as at present constituted, has existed nine years; and during that period has engaged in 102 Matches — of which it has won 74, lost 24 and drawn 4. . . . Such results require little comment.'

91. **La Clef du Cricket,** *ou courte explication de la marche et des principales règles de ce jeu; par 'An Old Stump'* [presumably Abel Kidd] *M.P.C.C.* [Privately printed.] *Paris, 1864.* 22pp. The statutes of the Paris Cricket Club demanded 'sociabilité, discipline, sang-froid, sang-froid et encore sang-froid, décision, promptitude et sûreté du coup d'oeil, vigilance, agilité, force et santé voilà les qualités que

demande et que donne le Cricket', and were signed by T. H. Sparks, treasurer and honorary secretary. The Paris Club produced several issues of pamphlets listing members etc, starting in 1863.

92. **Rules and Regulations of the Mauritius Cricket Club.** *1864.* 39pp. Major Van Straubenzee offered bats to the Club which were to be played for during the season by attaining the highest score.

93. **The cricketer's almanack, for the year 1864,** *being bissextile or leap year, and the 28th of the reign of Her Majesty Queen Victoria, containing the laws of cricket, as revised by the Marylebone Club; the first appearance at Lord's and number of runs obtained by many cricketing celebrities; scores of 100 and upwards, from 1850 to 1863; extraordinary matches; all the matches played between the Gentlemen and Players, and the All England and United Elevens, with full and accurate scores taken from authentic sources; etc. etc. London: Published and sold by John Wisden & Co. at their Cricketing and British Sports Warehouse, 2, New Coventry St., Haymarket, W. One shilling. W. H. Crockford, Greenwich. 1864.* So much has been said and written about Wisden's almanack that it needs little elaboration here. It should suffice to point bibliophiles in the direction of the definitive 'History of Wisden' by L. E. S. Gutteridge which was included in the 100th edition in 1963.

There have been two facsimile editions of the years 1864–1878; and two printed indexes, firstly by Rex Pogson, covering the editions 1864–1943, and more recently by Derek Barnard, for the period 1864–1984. E. L. Roberts compiled an index, which exists in typescript, of special articles, 'Cricketers of the Year', principal obituaries and statistical records, entitled **What's in Wisden, 1899–1937.**

Two issues of Wisden appeared in the years 1889–95, 1897–99 and 1901–02. E. K. Brown, the doyen of cricket booksellers, has intimated to the present writer that he may have seen second issues for other years as well.

For most years since 1950, John Arlott has reviewed annual additions to cricket's bookshelves. Prior to that, in 1938–42 and also in 1950, there appeared lists of books in print.

94. **John Lawrence's handbook of Cricket in Ireland:** *compiled and edited by J. T. H.*[urford]. *Publ. John Lawrence, Dublin.* This annual, comprising 16 issues, covers the seasons 1865–81. The last

volume, published in 1882, deals with both the 1880 and the 1881 seasons. It is difficult to find a complete run.

95. **Cardinal jottings and tottings: an account of two matches played by the Cardinal C. C.** *Marbury, Whitchurch, Shropshire, 1865.* 50pp. The account describes the Cardinal Cricket Club's games against Cheshire and Cheshire Colts in August 1865.

96. **A week's cricket: a rhyming record of the doings of a Liverpool eleven in Shropshire and neighbouring counties.** *Liverpool.* [c. 1865.] *Printed by the wish of the* [Anfield] *Eleven.* 33pp. Also included are the scores of games at Wrexham, Overton, Oswestry, Ellesmere, Whitchurch, Hawkstone and Shrewsbury. An introductory verse demonstrates how times have changed:

> Among the suburbs of our famous town
>   Is one called Anfield, small and unpretending,
> And not as yet of very great renown,
>   But rapidly increasing and extending,
> Intensely loyal, Tory to the core,
>   Highly respectable and nothing more.

97. **The Canterbury Cricket Week:** *an authentic narrative of the origin and career of the institution; including the programmes of The Old Stagers' Performances, with the original Prologues, Epilogues, etc. spoken at each season. Dedicated by permission to the Old Stagers, I. Zingari, and the Wandering Minstrels. Volume First. Canterbury; printed and published by William Davey, 1865.* ix + 86pp. The Canterbury cricket week originated with the Beverley Cricket Club, which was founded in 1835. Beverley C. C. later became the East Kent Club. Festive entertainment included dinners, balls and amateur theatricals at night; and cricket, complete with marquees, bunting and a band conducted by 'Herr' Felix, by day. The cricket week was linked closely to the ventures of I Zingari, which club had started life at the Blenheim Hotel, Cambridge. One of I Zingari's regulations was 'that the entrance be nothing, and the annual subscription do not exceed the entrance.'

The superbly produced book, which sports a coloured decorative half-title page, sepia photographs and gilt edges, was delayed in its preparation and costly to compile. There was insufficient financial support to produce the proposed second volume. Unless that second volume happened to reach a draft stage and lies somewhere forgotten,

101

the nearest one can get to appreciating its potential is to scan the ten I Zingari scrapbooks, which contain cuttings, drawings and engravings and were once the property of John Loraine Baldwin, a joint founder of the Club. The first of these volumes covers the tours and events which took place between 1845 and 1850, within the period covered by Davey's 'Canterbury Cricket Week', which is mainly concerned with the years 1843-51.

E. Milton Small produced **Canterbury Cricket Week, 1842-1891, its origin, career and jubilee** (1891, printed by J. A. Jennings), which had two succeeding issues, and H. W. Warner told **The Story of Canterbury Cricket Week** in a booklet printed by the same firm in 1960. Warner had also written **A History of Beverley Cricket Club,** which had been published in 22 pages the previous year and covered the period 1835-1959.

98. **Cricketana,** *by the author of 'The cricket-field'. James Pycroft. Longman, Green, Longman, Roberts and Green, London, 1865.* vi + 238pp. There are 13 chapters, which comment on such subjects as the early London clubs, I Zingari, the two 'All England XIs', public school matches and much else. A second edition came out in the same year. The book was put together from a series of papers contributed to the periodical 'London Society' in 1863 and 1864.

99. **Cricket: its theory and practice,** *by Capt. Crawley. (Chambers Useful Handbooks). George Frederick Pardon. Chambers, 1865.* viii + 72pp. This work was reproduced in a number of editions, the last being issued in 1889.

100. **Cricketers' handbook.** *James Banks. John Heywood, Manchester, 1865.* xvi + 45pp. The handbook lists principal clubs in England, Ireland and Scotland. Banks, who acted as compiler and editor, produced a much enlarged handbook for 1866, which ran to 184 pages and was published by the 'Cricketers News' office.

101. **The champion cricketer's guide and companion:** *containing a plan for the Cricket Field showing where you are to stand, etc . . . the whole art of cricket and everything a learner will require to know to make him a perfect cricketer. R. March & Co. St. James Walk, London.* [c. 1865.] 32pp. A number of issues were produced, containing slight re-arrangements on the title page. March also produced **The Young Cricketer's Companion** (c. 1870), which consists of 19 pages.

THE

Canterbury Cricket Week.

An Authentic Narrative of the Origin and Career of the Institution ;

Including the Programmes of

The Old Stagers' Performances,

With the Original

PROLOGUES, EPILOGUES, &c.,

Spoken at each Season.

Dedicated by Permission to the

Old Stagers, J Zingari, and the Wandering Minstrels.

Volume First.

Canterbury :
Printed and Published by William Davey.

1865.

See item 97

102. **Cricket, and how to play it:** *with the rules of the Marylebone Club. (The Champion Handbooks). John Wisden. Darton and Hodge.* [1866 ?] 62pp. Three mostly revised editions followed, using Wisden's name, each with a different publisher. Robert Abel took over the mantle in 1894 and 1895.

103. **Cricket:** *(Warne's Bijou Books) by Frederic*[k] *Wood. Warne, 1866.* 96pp. There was another edition in 1868, with which the series was described as 'The Bijou Book of Out-door Amusements'.

104. **Jerks in from Short-Leg** *by Quid* [R. A. Fitzgerald]. *Illustrated by W. H. du Bellew, Esq. London, 1866. Harrison, 59, Pall Mall, S.W. Printed by Harrison & Sons, St. Martins Lane.* iii + 137pp. Some fairly advanced humour for the time is provided by a man who was to become Hon. M. C. C. Secretary.

105. **Guide to the Cricket Ground.** *George H. Selkirk. Macmillan, 1867.* vii + 132pp. This rare but useful handbook explores many avenues of cricket. It contains a large folding facsimile scoring sheet.

106. **Scores of the principal cricket matches played by Cheltenham College;** *edited by an Old Collegian. Cheltenham, 1868. Darter.* 95pp. The 'principal' scores are principally of interest locally and to devotees of public school cricket.

107. **Cricket: Reminiscences of the Old Players and Observations on the Young Ones.** *By the author of 'The Cricket Field'. James Pycroft. 1868.* 22pp. There is intriguing gossip about familiar and unfamiliar material. This item is extremely scarce.

   Pycroft also wrote two volumes of **Oxford Memories: a retrospect after fifty years in 1886,** which, as is to be expected, contained remembrances of cricket. The game finds a place as well in his **Elkerton Rectory,** which is the second part of an autobiography entitled 'Twenty Years in the Church' (1860; later editions appeared in 1860 and 1861, and a reprint in 1862). His writings on cricket are also to be seen in other compilations: Frederick Wood's **Beeton's Cricket Book** (c. 1866; second edition 1869) and **Table Talk** (no date).

   Pycroft was a disciple of what is known as 'muscular Christianity', which is immediately obvious when one reads his occasional cricket offering to 'Boy's Own' and other youthful papers.

108. **The Theory and practice of cricket from its origin to the present time;** *with critical and explanatory notes upon the laws of the game, by 'Bat'* [Charles Box]. *Warne, 1868.* ix + 165pp. There was another issue in the same year, with a slightly revised title-page.

109. **Scottish cricketer's annual and guide** *edited by Percival King. P. King, Edinburgh.* The annual ran to 18 volumes (1870/71 to 1888/89). Vol. V covered 1874-76. An incomplete run, missing three volumes, sold for £150 recently at auction.

About this period, J. C. Stewart compiled **Stewart's Cricket Calendar** (1875-99), which was produced in Edinburgh and Manchester.

110. **Cricket: its theory and practice.** *Chas. Ward. Heckmondwike, Yorkshire. 1870.* 22pp. Another edition (c. 1885) consisted of 29 pages. Ward produced **The cricketer's guide: a complete manual...** in 1877, which was reproduced twice, firstly in 1883 and then a year later, with the addition of three sections. One of those sections, **An Essay on Cricket,** was issued separately as a five-page pamphlet in the same year (1884) and it, too, was produced about the same time with additions 'School cricket hints', 'Reverie on cricket' etc., comprising 32 pages in all.

In 'The Cricketer's Guide', Ward, who describes himself as a cricket implement merchant for home and exportation (the front cover shows exterior and interior views of a warehouse) enjoins: 'Play in earnest. Never let yourself degenerate into trifling or folly. A passing joke, or a little fun is unobjectionable and may serve to keep up good feeling; but a habit of laughing at others, shouting to distant fielders, running about, or leaping are exceedingly destructive to good play. The crack elevens play in silence.'

111. **Cricket Gossip.** *On Cricket and Cricketers. No.1. W. G. Grace Esq. by an Old Stump. Conversation between two old cricketers from the North and South of England at Lord's Ground, the meeting being the Gentlemen versus Players, July 3, 1871, and at Kennington Oval, July 6, 7, 8, 1871. Printed Kaygill and Rowe. Kentish Town.* 'Cricket Gossip' is a poem, which was published by the M.C.C. for the benefit of the author.

112. **The Whole Art of Cricket,** *with instructions how to bat and bowl and directions to wicket keeper, long stop, short slip, and each member of the cricket field by the late Fuller Pilch. Together with*

See item 112

the laws of cricket as laid down by the Marylebone Club. London. [c. 1875.] *G. Ingram, 124, Old St., St. Luke's, E.C.* 8pp. The wording on the title page, as given above, appears in the second edition. It was adapted with slight modification from that of the first edition, which had been published in about 1870 by W. S. Fortey. Pilch had died in May of that year.

113. **An account of a cricket match: "Public Schools" (Eton, Harrow and Winchester) versus "Private Schools" (Miss Tims's Pupils) played at Calcutta, on the 4th and 5th February, 1870.** *R. J. the Author, Calcutta, 1870.* 19pp. The account, which is entirely in verse, is one of the earliest cricket publications from the Indian subcontinent. In 1883, another extraordinary publication, entitled **Goa Growler**, 'a journal of no pretensions, no politics and no principles', was published by Duftur Ashkana as a memento of cricket matches played on board BISN Company's vessel 'SS Goa' during a voyage from London to Karachi and Bombay.

114. **Echoes from old Cricket Fields;** *or, sketches of cricket and cricketers from the earliest history of the game to the present time. Frederick Gale. London, Simpkin, Marshall & Co., 1871.* xii + 112pp. The book includes 'Twenty golden rules for young Cricketers', which had been produced as a separate booklet in 1869 and for which Gale acknowledges his indebtedness to 'Felix', who provided eight pages of notes. 'Echoes from old Cricket Fields' was published in a revised edition by the firm of Nutt in 1896; while the first edition was reprinted by S.R. Publishers of Wakefield in 1972, together with a foreword by John Arlott.

Gale's work is out of favour at the present time: his pontifical, righteous and rolling style of writing reads somewhat strangely for eyes accustomed to a modern page, yet his ever-present, if long-winded, humour is shown in several skits involving cricket and in a number of political squibs. John Bowyer, the old Surrey player, was the fortunate beneficiary of the cricketing skits: The 'Mitcham Illustrated Birthday Newspaper' (17 June 1871), 'The Alabama Claims' (1872) and 'Mr. Pepys on cricket' (1873).

An early burlesque of 1854, revealing Gale's public school involvement in cricket, had been privately printed in Latin text, 'In memoriam gloriosam ludorum Etoniensuum, Harroviensuum, Wykehamicorumque, nuper intermissorum . . .' It bemoaned the discontinuation of Winchester's matches at Lord's against Harrow and Eton. At more or less the same time, he had produced **The Public School Matches, and those we meet there** (pages 152 and 153, which contain the piece **De Catulo Pertinaci,** can also be found offprinted as a separate publication), which was coupled with **Ups and Downs of a Public School** when issued next in 1867. The edition of 1896 was titled **The Public School Cricket Matches of forty years ago.**

Further offerings were a memoir, **The Life of the Hon. Robert Grimston** (1885), and **The Game of Cricket** (1887), which had a second edition in the following year. A visit to Duke's cricket-ball factory had inspired a fanciful piece **About an old cricket ball,** which was offprinted as a 10-page pamphlet in 1882, after it had appeared as an article in 'Baily's Magazine'.

Cricket inevitably found a place in a few general sporting books with which Gale was involved, and the slimmest and scarcest of these is **Sports at High Elms, 1859 to 1875.** The Farnborough side at Sir John Lubbock's home are featured in descriptions that suggest country-house cricket at its best.

115. **1872 International Cricket Fete Official Hand-book,** *containing the programme of arrangements during the visit of the English Gentlemen Eleven to Philadelphia, together with the names and standing of the players and a variety of useful and entertaining matter relating to the game of cricket; also a score sheet for the use of spectators. Published for the Committee of arrangements by J. B. Lippincott & Co., Philadelphia, September, 1872.* 68 numbered pp. The Hand-book contains several whimsical effusions, including 'Mediumistic — Shakspeare [*sic*] interviewed: he gives a full report of the great match in advance'. The useful and entertaining matter includes a couple of songs ('Bob Bowler and Dick Driver' and 'The Unlucky Cricketer') and directions on how to reach the cricket ground.

116. **Official Report on the International Cricket Fetes at Philadelphia in 1868 and 1872,** *including balance-sheets, together with a full account of the Visit of the English Gentlemen Cricketers by R. A. Fitz-Gerald, Esq. Captain of the Twelve; also "Cricket in America", "Cricket for School-Boys", and other interesting matter relating to the game. Published for the Committee by J. B. Lippincott & Co., Philadelphia, 1873.* 38pp. The title says it all, or nearly: there is

also a description of 'Cricket by Moonlight'. The committee consisted of Charles E. Cadwalader, Chris. Stuart Patterson, Albert A. Outerbridge, George M. Newhall and Fred C. Newhall.

117. **Wickets in the west;** *or the twelve in America. R. A. Fitzgerald. Tinsley. 1873.* ix + 336pp. Fitzgerald's side included A. N. Hornby, Lord Harris and W. G. Grace. One might be asked to pay twice as much for this book as for **Jerks in from Short-Leg** (q.v.); it is not too hard to find in the U.S.A.

118. **The Halifax Cricket Tournament.** *An Account of the visit of the American Twelve of Philadelphia to Halifax in August, 1874.* [Published for private circulation only.] *Philadelphia, J. B. Lippincott & Co., 1874.* 54pp. Four matches were played: America v. Canada; America v. England; England v. Canada; and Halifax v. All-Comers. America won both their matches by an innings, England beat Canada, and Halifax took the honours, appropriately, in the final game.
   There was also a four-page pamphlet issued detailing the fixtures, prizes, rules and conditions.

119. **The rise, progress and vicissitudes of cricket in Herefordshire since its introduction to the county.** *Hereford Times, 1874.* 62pp. This work originally appeared as a series of articles in the 'Hereford Times'. 'The late Mr. Richard Jones Powell of Hinton near Hereford . . . was one of the first men to bring cricket into any note in this county.'

120. **The English Game of Cricket:** *comprising a digest of its origin, character, history and progress, together with an exposition of its laws and language. By Charles Box. Author of "The Cricketer's Manual", "Reminiscences of Celebrated Players", "Essays on the Game", "Songs and Poems", "Theory and Practice of Cricket", etc. London, 1877. "The Field" Office, 346, Strand.* x + 496pp. This archetypal Victorian tome tends today to be underrated. However, Box's scholarly dissertation covers such a wide aspect of cricket that the book is often found to be a useful reference for more obscure as well as for much-examined topics.

121. **Cricket as now played by Frederick D'Arros Planche and Baseball and Rounders** *by Captain Crawley, author of 'The Billiard Book' etc., etc. (Captain Crawley's Handbooks of Out-door Games).*

London, 1877. Ward, Lock and Co., Warwick House, Dorset Buildings, Salisbury Sq. E.C. viii + 120pp. Cricket forms the subject of the bulk of this book, which is listed first in a series of seven handbooks of outdoor games. Rawdon Crawley signs the Preface with style: 'Captain Unattached', Megatherium Club, Canterbury Week, 1877. There was another issue in 1892 which contained a few additions.

122. **Cricket as it should be played,** *with the rules of the Marylebone Club, and practical directions for amateurs. Ex-Captain* [pseudonym]. *(Ward and Lock's Sixpenny Handbooks).* Ward, Lock. [c. 1878.] 93pp. Other editions were issued, terminating in 1894. The contents are virtually identical to those of the cricket section in the previous item.

Ward, Lock and Tyler had brought out **The Adventures of a cricket ball** *with the laws and practice of cricket* by 'An Old Boy' in 1860; it contained 66 pages.

123. **Comicalities of the cricket field;** *with the compliments of the Peninsular Cricket Club. C. Browne Calvert. Detroit, Michigan, 1878.* Broadsheet. Two editions were published in England by Hurst of Sheffield (in 1878 and 1884); and in the early 1890s Calvert's illustrations were incorporated in a short chronicle entitled **The Comic Side of Cricket,** which was put together by Joseph Taylor under the auspices of the Detroit Athletic Club.

124. **Sussex county cricket scores from 1855–1878.** *George Ewbank.* [Privately printed in India.] *1878.* ii + 288pp. Major George Ewbank was the eldest son of the Rev. George Ewbank of Brighton. When he was stationed in India with his regiment, he compiled the scores for his own amusement. They were set and printed on a small hand machine by Major Anstruther. Apparently the book is a limited edition of only four copies, two of which are in the library at Lord's. A third sold at a recent Phillips auction for a hammer price of £180, and the fourth. . . . Where can that be?

125. **Sussex cricket past and present,** *by an old Sussex Cricketer. Charles Francis Trower. Alex Rivington, Lewes, 1879.* 60pp. 'Sussex cricket past and present' was an extension of Trower's essay 'On the archaeology of Sussex cricket', which had been published in **Sussex Archaeological Collections** the previous year.

Some recollections of cricket *Bibliographical Notes on Early Books*

126. **Some recollections of cricket.** *Lord Charles James Fox Russell. H. G. Fisher, High St., Woburn, 1879.* 39pp. According to A. D. Taylor, there were only 12 copies printed. Russell's 'little extravagance' was reprinted in a limited numbered edition of 100 for J. W. McKenzie, with an introduction by John Arlott, in 1979. The original edition contains: a dedication page to the Hon. Frederick Ponsonby and the Hon. Robert Grimston; the 'Harrow Classic' poem following the title page, on which is quoted Byron's verse on 'cricket's manly toil'; a preface; 'A Dream of the Past' (reprinted from 'Baily's Magazine'); 'Round-arm recollections' (reprinted from 'Baily's Magazine'); 'Lord's and Prince's, 1872'; 'Bedfordshire Cricket' (a circular in aid of B.C.C., reprinted from 'The Bedfordshire Mercury' of 9th August 1878); 'National testimonial to W. G. Grace' (an address delivered at Lord's on 22nd July 1879).

Russell, who was the sixth son of the sixth Duke of Bedford, was President of M.C.C. in 1835, sometime MP for Bedfordshire, and Sergeant-at-Arms in the House of Commons. He produced another tiny booklet on cricket in 1889, which was again limited to twelve copies (the number was authenticated by Russell): **Cricket, 1757–1889** contains the notice 'Opening of the Flitwick Recreation Ground 15th July 1889 and written for the Flitwick Cricket Club, 1889.' There are also references to cricket in a third of his booklets, **Some Recollections of the Chase,** and possibly also in **A Horn of Chase** (1886), which was a privately printed edition of 36 copies, containing a collection of eight pieces on hunting, that Russell said was only for use as prizes at a local dog show.

Russell also wrote on the game in his book of essays, **Woburn Echoes** (1881), in **Cricket, a popular handbook on the game** *by Dr. W. G. Grace, Rev. J. Pycroft, Frederick Gale and other well-known veteran authorities* (1887), and in magazine articles with such musings in his old age as ''Tis Sixty Years Since' (1885).

Whilst concentrating on the Bedfordshire seat, one should notice a manuscript of **Woburn Cricket Scores,** which covers the period 1833-49 and was once in A. E. Winder's collection, and **Woburn Park: a fragment in rural rhyme,** by George Castleden, which was printed and published by S. Dodd of Woburn in 1839. The book is divided into three parts, of which the second is devoted to cricket; one line reads, 'here we resume our cricket war'. A second edition, from another publisher (T. Ward), in which 102 pages are added to the original 66, came out in 1840.

127. **The Irish Cricketers in The United States 1879:** *by One of them.* [H. Brougham.] *John Lawrence, 63, Grafton St., Dublin. M. H. Gill & Son, 60, Upper Sackville St., Dublin. W. Kent & Co., Paternoster Row, London. 1880.* iv + 103pp. This colourful account in 35 chapters has an appendix from the New York Herald of 12th September 1879.

128. **St. Ivo and the Ashes:** *a correct, true and particular history of the Hon. Ivo Bligh's crusade in Australia by R. D. Beeston, illustrated by M. C. B. Massie 1882–3. Melbourne, 1883. Australian Press Agency. Albert S. Manders & Co., 91, Little Collins Street, East.* 23pp. The delightfully light-hearted report by Beeston (late Bengal Staff Corps) is complemented by humorous pen-and-ink sketches from Massie (late 13th Light Dragoons), and is much sought-after.

  A limited edition of 75 copies, with a foreword by John Arlott and the record of the 1882–83 tour of Australia by English cricketers (reprinted from Wisden's Almanack), was produced by J. W. McKenzie in 1978.

129. **The Ladies' Guide to Cricket** *by a Lover of both with a glossary of technical terms and cricket slang and the laws of cricket. 1883. Printed at the Freeman's Journal Office, Auckland.* 40pp. + errata slip. 'Two ladies exploring the dark continent of cricket . . .' were the subject of a prolonged joke before chauvinism was heard of.

  A pencilled annotation on the fly-leaf suggests that there is only one known copy. Maybe more await discovery in dusty corners of New Zealand.

130. **Cricket Notes** *by the Hon. T. W. H. Pelham, M.A., Trinity College, Camb., Barrister-at-law, Inner Temple. Published Wyman and Sons, Gt. Queen St., W. C. 1886.* 16pp. Various sources give other dates for this publication. The author comments that 'these notes were submitted to several old and present University players who made valuable criticisms and suggestions which have in many cases been adopted.' In the section headed 'Batting', Pelham counsels, 'Always wear pads. Neglect of this rule leads to slovenly cricket.'

131. **The Log of the 'Old 'Un' from Liverpool to San Francisco (1886).** *William Clulow Sim. For private circulation, H. S. Eland, Exeter. 1887.* i + 30pp. This extremely scarce book provides an account of the tour by E. J. Sanders's team. Sim was the unofficial scorer.

  Sanders's scrapbook of his playing days was sold in the mid-1980s by J. W. McKenzie, the cricket bookseller.

THE IRISH CRICKETERS

IN

THE UNITED STATES

1879.

BY

ONE OF THEM.

DUBLIN.
JOHN LAWRENCE, 63, GRAFTON STREET.
M H GILL & SON. 50. UP: SACKVILLE ST
KENT. & CO. PATERNOSTER ROW LONDON.

PRICE ONE SHILLING.

See item 127

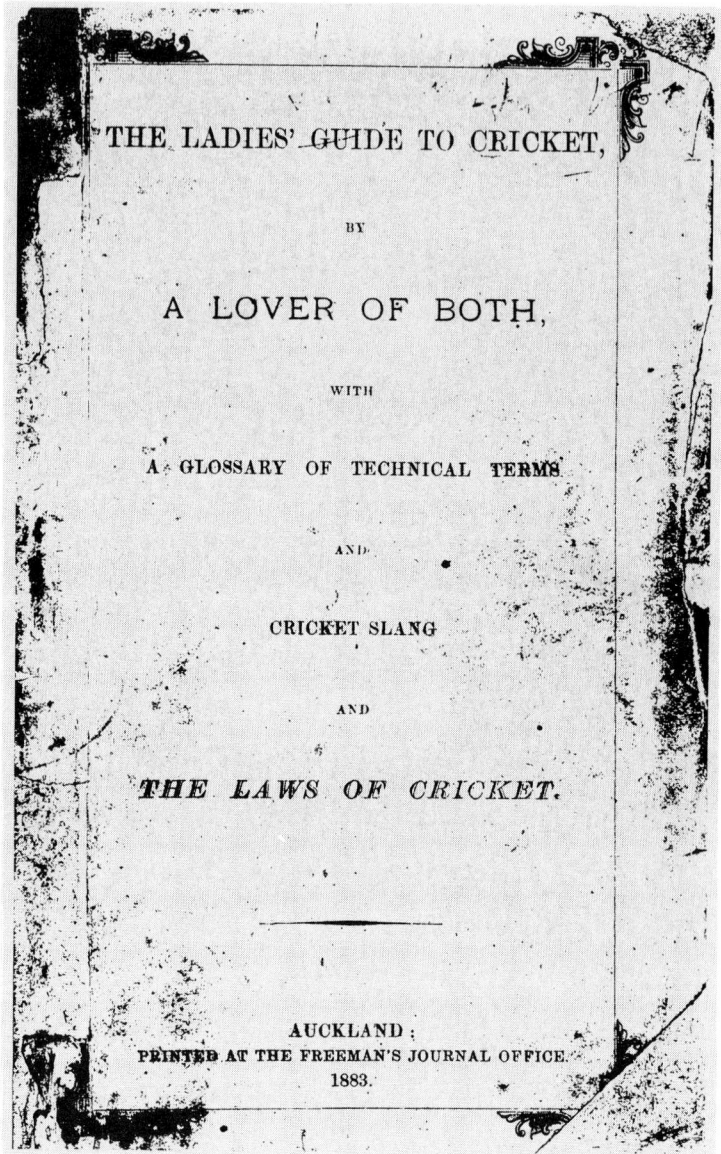

THE LADIES' GUIDE TO CRICKET,

BY

A LOVER OF BOTH,

WITH

A GLOSSARY OF TECHNICAL TERMS

AND

CRICKET SLANG

AND

THE LAWS OF CRICKET.

AUCKLAND:
PRINTED AT THE FREEMAN'S JOURNAL OFFICE.
1883.

See item 129

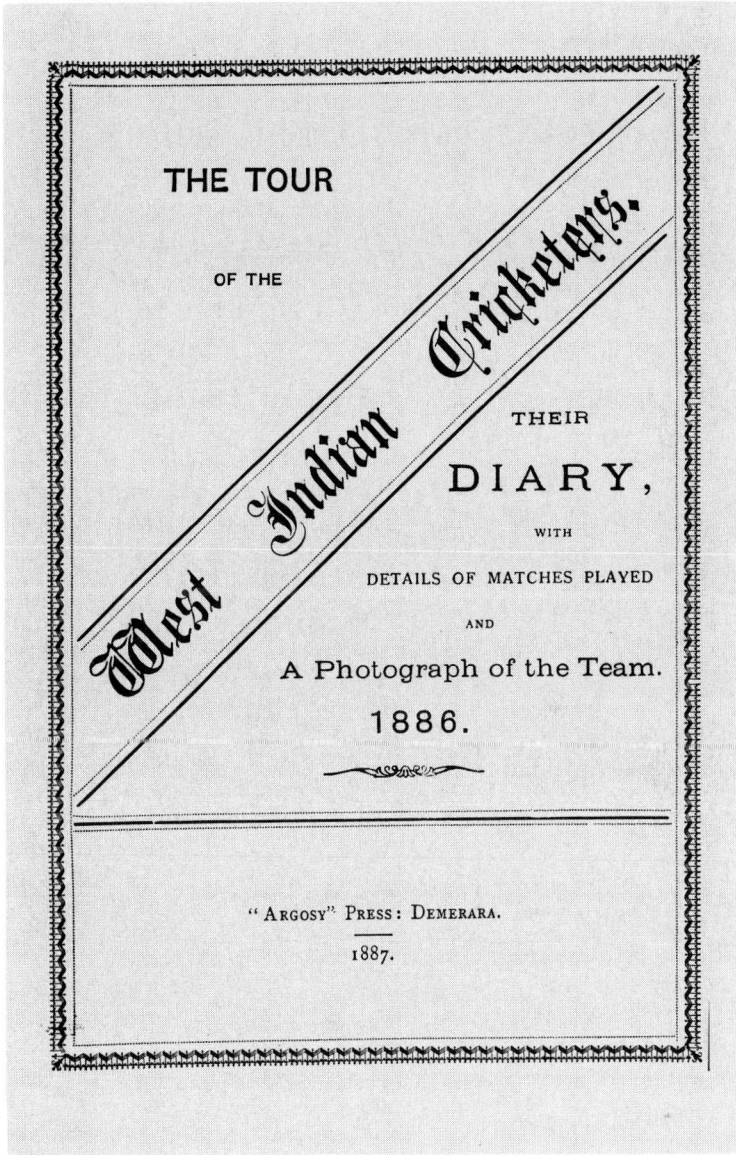

THE TOUR

OF THE

West Indian Cricketers.

THEIR

DIARY,

WITH

DETAILS OF MATCHES PLAYED

AND

A Photograph of the Team.

1886.

"ARGOSY" PRESS: DEMERARA.

1887.

See item 132

132. **The tour of the West Indian cricketers, August and September, 1886.** *Their Diary with details of Matches played and Photograph of the Team, 1886. Charles Guy Austin Wyatt and Lawrence R. Fyfe. 'Argosy' Press, 1887. Demerara.* 92pp. This account of the trip to North America was published after the tour had ended.

133. **Cricket across the sea;** *or, the wanderings and matches of the Gentlemen of Canada, by two of the Vagrants. Dyce Willcocks Saunders and George Goldwin Lindsay Smith. Murray, Toronto, 1887.* 223pp. The Gentlemen of Canada make a visit to England. This book is rare and therefore expensive: £300 was being asked for a copy in 1985.

134. **Early cricket in Ireland:** *a paper read before the Kingstown Literary and Debating Society on the 22nd February, 1888. Arthur Samuels. W. McGee for the Society. Dublin, 1888.* 34pp. A copy sold for £5 at the Goldman sale in 1966.

   One of the earliest references to cricket in Ireland is found in **Dermot and Cicely;** *or, the Irish gimblet, a tale in three canto's* [sic], *in the manner of Hudibras.* The 23 pages, containing a description of cricket in Munster, were printed by W. Trow, without Temple-Bar, in 1742.

135. **The log of a trip in Lord Sheffield's yacht 'Heloise' to Boulogne and back by 'One of the team'.** *Edwin J. Golding. Printed by C. Clarke, Haywards Heath, 1890.* 12pp. The log contains scores of matches played at Newhaven and Boulogne in July 1890. It is exceptionally difficult to procure a copy.

136. **The log of a trip in the Earl of Sheffield's yacht 'Heloise' to Torquay and back** *by 'E. J. G.' and 'W. M.' Printed by C. Clarke, Haywards Heath, 1890.* 14pp. This piece of *obscura* is even harder to find, if that is possible, than the preceding one.

   Sheffield was responsible for beautifully designed coloured menu cards composed for special functions, all now cherished collector's items. The text of his speech at the Australia Hotel in December 1891, mounted in a leather-bound folder opposite an ornate water-colour sketch of the Oval, was bought at auction recently for £130 (before the addition of commission and value added tax).

137. **The Cricket Guide intended for the use of young players** *containing a short but comprehensive account of the game embracing all the important rules and directions nicely arranged in due succession*

by Mohummud Abdullah Khan. Published at the Royal Printing Press, Lucknow, by the author's sincere friend, Mirza Alayar Beg. August, 1891. ii + 28pp. Khan has been called 'the Indian Nyren'; which is rather an overstatement. Having posed a question, 'What cricket is?', he proceeds to tell us the effect the sport can have, in charming idiosyncratic fashion:

> It is really a matter of deep regret and sorrow, that at a time when the game is so universal and common in every direction of the world, under the living canopy of heaven, very few are the thorough masters of its rules and regulations. Even those who are very good and noble (say next door to angels) turn so rash and inconsiderate at certain moments, that their brains lose the balance and begin to take fallacious fancies.
>
> It is surely not a difficult problem to be solved, for at a moment when their blood is at fever heat, their minds are in a chaos of tumult, they seem in field as if treading on a volcano; it is no reason why they should not boil over with rage, pick up quarrels with one another, and even look daggers at their own dearest friends and darlings.

138. **A History of Parsee Cricket** *(being a lecture delivered at the Framji Cowasji Institute, under the presidency of Dr. Blaney on the 10th December, 1892 by Manekji Kavasji Patel, Assistant Teacher, Fort High School, Bombay.* [Bombay, the author.] *Printed at the J. N. Petit Parsi Orphanage Captain Printing Press, 1892.* viii + 101pp. The book originally sold for 8 annas. There were a number of Parsee cricket publications around this time, including **An entertaining account of the Parsi Cricket Club's tours** by Peshtanji Jeevanji Master, issued by the Rising Star Printing Press in Gujerati text in 1892, **A chronicle of cricket amongst Parsees and the struggle Polo versus Cricket** by Shapoorji Sorabji (c. 1898), **Parsi Cricket** *with hints on bowling, batting, fielding, captaincy, explanation of laws of cricket, etc. etc.* by Mehrvanji Erachji Pavri (1901) and **Stray thoughts on Indian cricket** by J. M. Framjee Patel (1905). All these works were published in Bombay. In Calcutta in 1897, Thacker Spink published **Mayo College Cricket Matches** (covering the period 1875–95), a compilation by Herbert Sherring.

139. **Record of Lord Hawke's cricket team in India, 1892–93.** *Redin and Co., 16, Trinity St., Cambridge.* [c. 1893.] 28pp. This rare tour book contains a photograph of the team, an anonymous introduction, and full scores and final averages for the 23 matches.

140. **Kings of Cricket:** *reminiscences and anecdotes with hints on the game. Richard Daft. Arrowsmith, Bristol. Simpkin, Marshall, London. 1893.* xiv + 274pp. The introduction by Andrew Lang should be treasured. A subscriber's edition of 150 copies was produced by Tillotson of Bolton.

Daft was the leading batsman in the North of England for many years. An unpublished manuscript of **Richard Daft's English cricketers in Canada and the United States,** by Edwin Brown, is in the library at Trent Bridge. A second volume of Daft's reminiscences, edited by F. S. Ashley-Cooper, appeared posthumously under the title **A Cricketer's Yarns.**

In the same year as 'Kings of Cricket' was published, a 32-page pamphlet was issued of **Press Critiques** on the book, and also of **Cricket: past, present and future,** by W. G. Grace.

141. **Cricket** *by W. G. Grace. J. W. Arrowsmith, 11, Quay St., Bristol. Simpkin, Marshall, Hamilton, Kent & Co., Ltd., London. 1891.* xii + 512pp. A crown quarto édition de luxe was printed of 650 copies and also 10 presentation copies. Another edition was produced by Heinemann and Balestier of Leipzig the next year. A printed inscription by Grace reads, 'I think it right my readers should know that I have been much aided in the preparation of this book by my friend W. Methven Brownlee, who has worked with me over every page and thus helped me to place this history of cricket before lovers of Our National Game.'

142. **Bibliography of Cricket** *by Alfred J. Gaston. Ditchling Rise, Brighton, 1895. Printed for Private Circulation by D. B. Friend & Co., 77, Western Road, Brighton.* [Limited edition of 25.] 12pp. Gaston's was the first separately printed bibliography of cricket. He also supplied a bibliography for **Wisden's Almanack** in the years 1892, 1894, 1900 and 1923. There are in existence at least two copies in typescript of his bibliographical findings and also an offprint in paper covers of his contribution to Wisden in 1923.

Gaston was not only a dealer and collector, but also a prolific writer on cricket. Besides articles on 'Cricket books and their prices' for 'The Cricket Field', he compiled a number of publications, such as **A short biography of Walter A. Humphreys, the famous Sussex Cricketer** and **Pocket Synopsis of Sussex Cricket,** as well as benefit pamphlets for players (Jesse Hide, Harry Butt, Fred Tate, G. R. Cox, E. H. Killick and others), **The History of Cricket in**

BIBLIOGRAPHY

OF CRICKET.

BY

ALFRED J. GASTON,

DITCHLING RISE, BRIGHTON,

1893.

Printed for Private Circulation by D. B. FRIEND & CO.,
77 Western Road, Brighton.

See item 142

PREFACE.

TO *ensure accuracy in*
detail, proof sheets of the

BIBLIOGRAPHY OF

CRICKET were submitted

to—

F. A. BROOKE, ARTHUR HAYGARTH,

E. B. V. CHRISTIAN, R. S. HOLMES,

A. L. FORD, T. PADWICK,

C. P. GREEN, J. B. PAYNE.

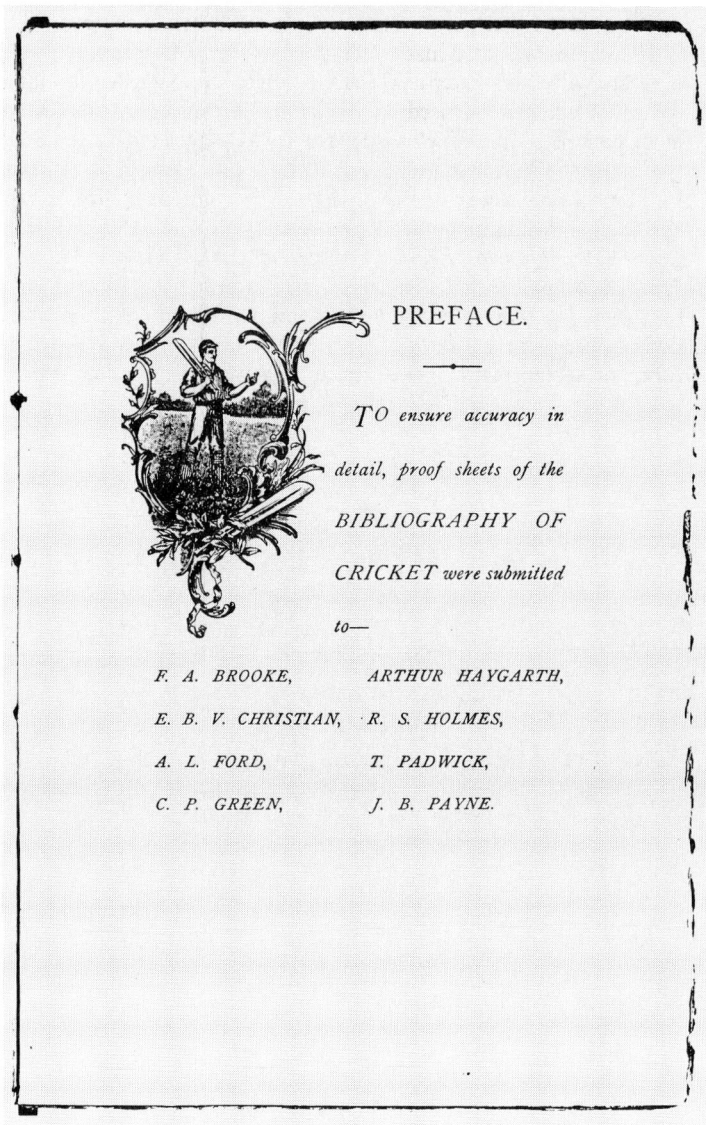

From Gaston's *Bibliography of Cricket*: see item 142.

Sussex (1898) and **Sussex County Cricket 1728–1923** (1923), which received four editions and was updated. An autograph edition of 100 copies was also made of **Sussex County Cricket.**

Gaston also kept busy as a dealer. He issued extensive catalogues, several of which advertised the cricket collections of friends who had died, such as Alfred Taylor and Thomas Padwick.

Finally, a bibliographical question-mark; one which some readers may be able to answer. On perusing J. W. Goldman's **Bibliography** (1937), the eye lights upon two entries assigned to Gaston: **Cricket, 1774–1842** (*Quarto. Private circulation*) and **Cricket Talks** (*12 copies only, private circulation*, 1920). Goldman's comment for the first item is, 'scarce' and for the second, 'like all private circulations — very scarce.' They are not entered in Padwick's **Bibliography,** nor, as far the present author can recall, has either appeared in post-war catalogues. Where are they now?

Only Twenty-five Copies of this
Bibliography printed

This Copy is Number

Signed

INDEX
of Cricket Books and their Authors

(*Note:* page numbers in **bold type** denote an illustration.)

About an old cricket ball (Gale, 1882), 108
An account of a cricket match: "Public Schools" (Eton, Harrow and Winchester) versus "Private Schools" (Miss Tims's Pupils) played at Calcutta, on the 4th and 5th February, 1870 (1870), 107
An account of all the cricket matches played between Eton and Winchester; Westminster and Charterhouse; Rugby and Marlborough; and Marlborough and Cheltenham (F. Lillywhite and Wisden, 1857), 96
The Adventures of a cricket ball (1860), 110
The American Cricketer (1877–1929), 39
American cricket manual (Chadwick, 1873 and later editions), 90
Annals of Cricket (Read, 1896), 38
Arlott, John, 40, 41, 43, 50, 73, 100, 107, 111, 112
Ashley-Cooper, F. S., 15, 38, 39, 62, 85, 86, 94, 118
The Athletic News, 39
Auckland Cricketers' Trip to the South in 1873–4, 89
Audley End Cricket book (1844), 71
The Australian Cricketer's Guide for 1856–7 (Fairfax, 1857), 86, **87**
Ayre's Cricket Companion (1902–31), 39

Banks, James, 102
The Barbados Cricketers' Annual (1894/95–1913/14), 39

Barber, G. A., 78
'Bat' (Charles Box), 34, 81, 97, 105, 109
Baxter, John, 18, 20, 23, 56, 59
Bayly, Capt. W., 99
Beadle's dime book of cricket (1860 and later editions), 90
Beeston, R. D., 112
Beeton's Cricket Book (Wood, 1866 and later editions), 104
Bentley, Henry, 23, 61
Bew, J., 15, 50
Bibliography of Cricket (Gaston, 1895), 118, **119, 120, 121**
Bibliography of Cricket (Goldman, 1937), 56, 70, 121
A Bibliography of Cricket (Padwick, 1977), 44, 55, 61, 67, 82, 121
Boston Cricket Club (1809), 55
Bowen, Rowland, 81, 82, 89
Box, Charles ('Bat'), 34, 81, 97, 105, 109
Boxall, Thomas, 18, 20, 23, 55
Bramshill Cricket Club (1810), 56
Brecon Town and Garrison Cricket Club (1850), 84
Britcher, Samuel, 17, 18, 55
Brodribb, Gerald, 34, 78
Burden, James W., 84
Burnby, John, 15, 50

The cabinet: a repository of facts, figures and fancies relating to the voyage of the "Great Britain" S.S. from Liverpool to Melbourne, with the Eleven of All England (Reid, 1862), 97
Calvert, C. Browne, 110

The Canadian cricketers' guide and review of the past season (1858 and later editions), 90
The Canterbury Cricket Week (1865), 101, **103**
Canterbury Cricket Week, 1842–1891, its origin, career and jubilee (Small, 1891), 102
Cardinal jottings and tottings: an account of two matches played by the Cardinal C.C. (1865), 101
Cardus, Sir Neville, 41, 50
Catalogue of Cricket Literature (Taylor, 1906), 25, 55
The champion cricketer's guide and companion (March, c. 1865), 102
A chronicle of cricket amongst Parsees and the struggle Polo versus Cricket (Sorabji, c. 1898), 117
Chronicles of Cricket (1888), 71, 73
Clark, William Mark, 30, 73, 74, 76
Clarke, Charles Cowden, 27, 63
La Clef du Cricket (Kidd, 1864), 99
Cole, William, 24, 61
Colney Hatch Cricket Club (Baldock, 1856), 89
Comicalities of the cricket field (Calvert, 1878 and later editions), 110
The Comic Side of Cricket (Taylor), 110
A Correct Account of all the Cricket Matches played by the Nottingham Old Cricket Club, from 1771 to 1829 inclusive (North, 1830), 62
A correct account of all the cricket matches played by the Ripon Cricket Club, 1813–36 (Gatenby, 1837), 66
A Correct Account of all the Cricket Matches which have been played by the Marylebone Club and all other Principal Matches for the year 1786 to 1822 inclusive (Bentley, 1823 and later editions), 23, **60**, 61
Crawley, Capt. Rawdon, 102, 109, 110
Cricket periodical, 39
Cricket (W. G. Grace, 1891 and later editions), 118

Cricket (Wood, 1866 and later editions), 104
Cricket, 1774–1842 (Gaston), 121
Cricket, 1757–1889 (Russell, 1889), 111
Cricket: a collection of all the grand matches of cricket, played in England, within twenty years (Epps, 1799), 18, **19**, 55
Cricket across the sea (Saunders and Smith, 1887), 116
Cricketana (Pycroft, 1865), 28, 102
Cricket, and how to play it (Wisden, 1866 and later editions), 104
Cricket: an heroic poem ('Dance'—Love, 1744), **14**, 15, 47
Cricket, a popular handbook on the game by Dr. W. G. Grace, Rev. J. Pycroft, Frederick Gale and other well-known veteran authorities (1877), 111
Cricket as now played by Frederick D'Arros Planche and Baseball and Rounders (Crawley, 1877 and later editions), 109
The Cricket Bat and how to use it ('Felix'—Wanostrocht, 1861 and later editions), 78
The Cricket Chronicle for the season 1863 (Bayly, 1863), 99
The Cricketer, 39, 42, 59
The cricketer's almanack (Wisden, 1864 and later editions), 7, 35, **36**, 37, 44, 97, 100, 112, 118
Cricketers' annual (James Lillywhite, 1872 and later editions), 37, 82
The Cricketer's Chronicle (Burden), 84
The cricketer's companion (Denison, 1844 and later editions), 33, 71, **72**
Cricketer's Companion (Lillywhite, 1865 and later editions), 37, 82
The Cricketer's Guide (Dean, c. 1836 and later editions), 66
The cricketer's guide: a complete manual . . . (Ward, 1877 and later editions), 105
The cricketer's guide: a complete manual of the game of cricket (Heywood, 1863 and later editions), 99

Early Books on Cricket

Cricketers' handbook (Banks, 1865 and later editions), 102
The Cricketer's Handbook (Clark, c. 1845 and later editions), 30, 73, **74, 75**
Cricketer's handbook: a complete guide to field sports in general (Kerton, 1852), 86
The Cricketer's Hand-Book (Tyas, 1838 and later editions), 30, **31,** 67
The Cricketers' Manual (Dipple, c. 1850), 84
The cricketers' manual, for 1848 ('Bat'—Box, 1848 and later editions), 34, **80,** 81
The Cricketer's Manual for the Border Counties, 85
The Cricketers of My Time (Nyren, 1833), **26,** 27, 63, **64**
Cricketer's own register: score sheets and instructions (F. Lillywhite and Ward, 1865), 96
The Cricketer's Pocket Companion, 24, 59
The Cricketer's Pocket Companion (Cole, 1826), 24, 61
The Cricketer's Register for 1833, 63
A Cricketer's Yarns, 118
The Cricket Field, 118
The Cricket Field; or the history and the science of cricket (Pycroft, 1851 and later editions), **2** (facing title page), 28, **29,** 85, 97, 102, 104
Cricket Gossip, 105
The Cricket Guide intended for the use of young players (Khan, 1891), 116
Cricket Highways and Byways (Ashley-Cooper, 1927), 38
Cricket: its theory and practice (Crawley, 1865 and later editions), 102
Cricket: its theory and practice (Ward, 1870 and later editions), 105
Cricket made easy (1857 and later editions), 89
The Cricket Matches between Harrow and Eton and Harrow and Winchester from 1818–1852, 67
Cricket Notes (Clark, Bolland and Saunders, 1851), 85

Cricket Notes (Pelham, 1886), 112
Cricket: past, present and future (W. G. Grace, 1893), 118
The cricket player's pocket companion (Mayhew and Baker, 1859), 30, 90, **91**
The Cricket Quarterly, 71, 81, 82, 89
Cricket: Reminiscences of the Old Players and Observations on the Young Ones (Pycroft, 1868), 104
Cricket Scores and Biographies of Celebrated Cricketers, from 1746 [15 vols.] (F. Lillywhite/Haygarth, 1862), 33, 37, 94, **95**
Cricket: Sketches of the Players (Denison, 1846), 33, 73
Cricket Talks (Gaston, 1920), 121
Cricket: the full scores of all the All-England, United, County and first-class eleven a side matches played in the season 1862 (Thorp, 1862), 97, **98**
The Cricket Tutor (Pycroft, 1862 and later editions), 28, **97**
Cricket: with full instructions how to learn and how to play (F. Lillywhite, 1862), 96
Crossley, J. S., 70
The Cryketeers (Williams, 1790), 15, 50, **52, 53**

Daft, Richard, 38, 118
Richard Daft's English cricketers in Canada and the United States (Brown), 118
Dance, James, 13, 47
The Dawn of Cricket (Waghorn), 94
Denison, William, 33, 71, 73
Descriptive key to Mason's national print of a cricket match between Sussex and Kent, 1849 (Gambert, 1849), 81
A digest of cricketing facts and feats appertaining to the year 1862 (Platts, 1863), 97
The Doings of the eleven . . . ('Felix'—Wanostrocht; 2 volumes, 1851 and 1852), 78

Driver, Thomas, 70
Duncombe, Rev. John, 15, 50

Early cricket in Ireland (1888), 116
Echoes from old Cricket Fields (Gale, 1871 and later editions), 107
1872 International Cricket Fete Official Hand-book (1872), 108
The English Cricketers' Trip to Canada and The United States (F. Lillywhite, 1860), **92, 93,** 94
The English Game of Cricket (Box, 1877), 34, 109
An entertaining account of the Parsi Cricket Club's tours (Master, 1892), 117
Epps, W., 18, 55
An Essay on Cricket (Ward, 1884), 105
Established rules of the Goodwood Cricket Club (1813), 56, **57**
Ewbank, Major George, 110

Familiar Instructions for playing the noble Game of Cricket (Limbird, 1836 and later editions), 66
'Felix' (Nicholas Wanostrocht), 33, 34, 78, 81, 84, 86, 107
Felix on the bat ('Felix'—Wanostrocht, 1845 and later editions), 33, 78, 81
Fitzgerald, R. A., 37, 104, 108, 109

Gale, Frederick, 38, 70, 107
The Game at Cricket, As settled by the Several Cricket Clubs, Particularly that of the Star and Garter in Pall-Mall (Reeve, 1755), 30, 47
The Game of Cricket (Gale, 1887 and later editions), 108
Garrison Cricket Club (1816), 56, **58**
Gaston, Alfred, 7, 38, 96, 118, 121
Gauntlet's cricketers' record, 94
Golding, Edwin J., 116
Goldman, J. W., 24, 56, 66, 70, 78, 121
Goldwin, William, 12, 47
Grace, Edward Mills, 97
Grace, W. G., 38, 105, 111, 118

Grimston, Edward Harbottle, 25
Guide to the Cricket Ground (Selkirk, 1867), 104

Haandbog i cricket og langbold (1866), **88,** 89
The Halifax Cricket Tournament (1874), 109
The Hambledon Men (Lucas, 1907), 40, 50
The Handbook of Cricket (Routledge, 1862 and later editions), 97
Harrild, Robert, 18, 23, 55, 99
Haygarth, Arthur, 37, 94, 96
Headlam, Cecil, 38
Heywood, John, 99
A History of Beverley Cricket Club (Warner, 1959), 102
The History of Cricket in Sussex (Gaston, 1898), 118
A History of Parsee Cricket (1892), 117
How to Play Clarke ('Felix', 1852), 85
How to play cricket (Stevens, c. 1859), 94

The Illustrated Laws of Cricket as revised by The Marylebone Club, 1849 (Burden, 1849), 84
Imperial Cricket (Warner, 1912), 39
In Certamen Pilae (Goldwin, 1706), 12, **46,** 47
Instructions and rules for playing the noble game of cricket (Lambert, 1816), 20, **20, 21,** 23, 56
Instructions for playing the game of cricket (c. 1838), 66
The International Cricket Match played Oct. 1859 in the Elysian Fields at Hoboken on the ground of the St. George's Club (Irving, 1859), 90
The Invincible Cricket Guide (1895), 85
The Irish Cricketers in The United States 1879 (Brougham, 1880), 112, **113**

Jerks in from Short-Leg ('Quid'—Fitzgerald, 1866), 104, 109
The Journal of the Cricket Society, 89

Early Books on Cricket

The Kentish Cricketers (Burnby, 1773), 15, **49**, 50
Kerton, W. G., 86
Khan, Mohummud Abdullah, 117
Kidd, Abel, 43, 99
Kingscote, Henry Robert, 25
Kingscote Cricket Club (1822 and later editions), 25, 62
Kings of Cricket (Daft, 1893), 118
Knight, W. H., 35

The Ladies' Guide to Cricket (1883), 112, **114**
Lambert, William, 20, 23, 56, 59
Lansdown Cricket Club Matches (Peach, 1852), 85
John Lawrence's handbook of Cricket in Ireland, 100
Laws of cricket (1806), 55
The Laws of Cricket (Rait Kerr, 1950), 50
The Laws of Cricket, as revised and amended by the Mary-le-bonne Club (Barber, 1845), 76, **77**
Lillywhite, Fred, 28, 34, 35, 71, 82, 94, 96
Lillywhite, John, 28, 82, 90, 96
Lillywhite, William, 33, 82
James Lillywhite's Cricketer's Companion, 82
John and James Lillywhite's Cricketer's Companion, 82
Lillywhite's Illustrated hand-book of cricket (F. W. Lillywhite, 1844 and later editions), **32**, 33, 71
List of all the principal matches of cricket that have been played in the year (Britcher, 1790 and later editions), 17, **54**, 55
A List of Matches to be published in F. Lillywhite's Large Work of Cricket Scores from 1746 to 1856 inclusive (1857), 96
The log of a trip in Lord Sheffield's yacht 'Heloise' to Boulogne and back by 'One of the team' (Golding, 1890), 116
The log of a trip in the Earl of Sheffield's yacht 'Heloise' to Torquay and back (Golding, 1890), 116

The Log of the 'Old 'Un' from Liverpool to San Francisco (1866) (Sim, 1887), 112
Love, James, 13, 47
Lucas, E. V., 40, 50
Lyttelton, R. H., 38

The Manual of Cricket (Paterson, 1847), 34, 78, **79**
A manual of cricket and baseball (Mayhew and Baker, 1858), 30, 90
Masters, J., 24
A Match Diary 1824/5 (Grimston), 25
Matches of the Calcutta Cricket Club 1844–1854 (1854), 86
Matches of the Liverpool Cricket Club, 1847–64 (1865), 55
Matches of the Royston Cricket Club, 1855–1863 (Perkins, 1864), 99
Matches played by the Haileybury Cricket Club, 1840–51 (1852), 85
May, Percy, 38
Mayo College Cricket Matches (Sherring, 1897), 117
The Middle Ages of Cricket (Arlott, 1949), 73
Mitford, Rev. John, 28
Musae Juveniles (Goldwin, 1706), 12, **46**, 47

Natal Cricketers' Annual, 39, 89
The Noble Cricketers (Bew, 1778), 15, 50, **51**
The Noblest Game (Cardus and Arlott, 1969), 41, 50
North, W., 62
Nottingham cricket matches, from 1771 to 1853 (Sutton, 1853 and later editions), 86
Nyren, John, 24, 27, 28, 63

Official Report on the International Cricket Fetes at Philadelphia in 1868 and 1872 (1873), 108
Old-Time Cricket (Thomas), 47
The original and unrivalled Mosslake Field Cricket Society: rules and regulations (1807), 55

Padwick, E. W. (Tim), 7, 44, 55, 61, 62, 67, 81, 82, 89, 121
Pam-lu, Chess and Cricket (Warville, 1809), 25
Parsi Cricket (Pavri, 1901), 117
Paterson, Alexander D., 33, 78, 81
Pavilion Echoes from the South, 1884-5, 89
Peakodde, Bailzie, 63
Pelham, the Hon. T. W. H., 112
Penny illustrated guide to the cricket field (Maddick and Pottage, 1863), 99
Perkins, Henry, 99
Pocket Book of the Laws of Cricket (F. Lillywhite), 96
Pocket Synopsis of Sussex Cricket (Gaston), 118
Practical Hints on Cricket, for the direction and guidance of beginners (Gale, 1843 and later editions), 70
The principles of scientific batting (Pycroft, 1835 and later editions), 28, 63, **65**
The Public School Matches, and those we meet there (Gale), 108
The Public School Cricket Matches of forty years ago (Gale, 1896), 108
The Pump (Peakodde, 1835), 63
Pycroft, Rev. James, 27, 28, 63, 85, 97, 102, 104

The Queensland Cricketers' Guide and Annual for 1884-5, 89

Rait Kerr, R. S., 8, 33, 50, 59
Ranjitsinghi, 38
Read, W. W., 37, 38
Record of Lord Hawke's cricket team in India, 1892-93 (c. 1893), 117
Reeve, W., 30
The Register of Cricket for Hingham (Driver, 1844), 70
Regulations of the Cricket Club, Port Oratova, Tenerife 1826-28, 62
Reminiscences of the Old Players (Pycroft), 28
The rise, progress and vicissitudes of cricket in Herefordshire since its

introduction to the county (1874), 109
Roberts, E. L., 100
Routledge, Edmund, 97
Rules and Instructions for Playing at the Game of Cricket (Boxall, 1801 and later editions), 18, 20, **22**, 23, 55
Rules and regulations of the Harlequin Cricket Club, 70
Rules and regulations of the Isle of Wight Cricket Club (1839), 70
Rules and Regulations of the Mauritius Cricket Club (1864), 100
Rules and Regulations of the Mexican Union Cricket Club (1838), 67, **68**
Rules of Lynn Cricket Club (1833), 70
Rules of the Andover Cricket Club, 62
Rules of the Bangor Cricket Club, 84
Rules of the Haigh Colliery Cricket Club (1849), 81
Rules of the Old Westminster Cricket Club (1828), 62
Russell, Lord Charles James Fox, 111

St. Ivo and the Ashes (Beeston, 1883), 112
The scores of the Cricket matches played by Rugby School from the year MDCCCXXXI (Crossley, 1842 and later editions), 70
Scores of the principal cricket matches played by Cheltenham College (1868), 104
Scottish cricketer's annual and guide (King), 105
Selkirk, George H., 104
Shepheard, George, 50
A short account of the origin of the Kilkenny Cricket Club, and of its proceedings, in the years 1830-31 (1832), 63
A short biography of Walter A. Humphreys, the famous Sussex Cricketer (Gaston), 118
Sim, William Clulow, 112
A Sketch-book (Shepheard, c. 1790), 50
Small, E. Milton, 102
Some recollections of cricket (Russell, 1879), 111

South African Cricketers' Annual, 39, 89
The South African Cricketing Guide 1871–2, 89
Steel, A. G., 38
Stewart's Cricket Calendar, 105
The Story of Canterbury Cricket Week (Warner, 1960), 102
Stray thoughts on Indian cricket (Patel, 1905), 117
A succinct account of the Eleven of England, selected to contend in the great cricket matches of the north, for the year 1847 ('Felix'—Wanostrocht), 78
Surry Triumphant: or the Kentish-mens defeat (Duncombe, 1773), 15, 48, 50
Sussex County Cricket 1728–1923 (Gaston, 1923 and later editions), 121
Sussex county cricket scores from 1855–1878 (Ewbank, 1878), 110
Sussex cricket past and present (Trower, 1879), 110
Sutton, John Frost, 86

Taylor, Alfred D., 25, 38, 55, 97, 121
Ten thousand miles through India and Burma (Headlam, 1903), 38
The Theory and practice of cricket from its origin to the present time ('Bat'—Box, 1868), 34, 105
Thomas, P. F., 47
Thorp, Richard Clarke, 97
The Tournament Chronicle (1884 and later editions), 89
The tour of the West Indian cricketers, August and September, 1886 (Wyatt and Fyfe, 1887), 115, 116
La tranca: juego atletico (Williams, 1881), 89
Treatise on the Cut ('Felix'—Wanostrocht), 78
The trip to Australia: scraps from the diary of one of the twelve (Grace, 1864), 97

Trower, Charles Francis, 110
Turner, Thomas, 17
Tyas, Robert, 30, 67

Ups and Downs of a Public School (Gale, 1867), 108

Wanostrocht, Nicholas ('Felix'), 33, 34, 78, 81, 84, 86, 107
Warner, H. W., 102
Warner, Sir Pelham ('Plum'), 39
Warville, George Augustus, 25
A week's cricket: a rhyming record of the doings of a Liverpool eleven in Shropshire and neighbouring counties (c. 1865), 101
What's in Wisden, 1899–1937 (Roberts), 100
The Whole Art of Cricket (Pilch, c. 1870 and 1875), 105, 106
The Whole Art of Cricket and how to play it (c. 1840), 69, 70
The Whole Game of Cricket (Neal, c. 1844), 70
Wickets in the west (Fitzgerald, 1873), 37, 109
Wisden, John, 7, 28, 35, 96, 100, 104, 112
Wisden Cricket Monthly, 10
John Wisden's Cricketer's Notebook (1900–13), 39
With the M.C.C. to New Zealand (May, 1907), 38
Woburn Cricket Scores, 111
Wood, F., 104
Wykehamical Scores from the year 1825 (Cowburn, 1838 and later editions), 67

The Young Cricketer's Companion (March, c. 1870), 102
The Young Cricketer's Guide (F. Lillywhite, 1849 and later editions), 34, 82, 83
The Young Cricketer's Tutor (Nyren, 1833), 26, 27, 63, 64